Financial Reporting and Analysis

A beginner's guide

Dr. M. Imran Ahsan Dhothar

Preface

Do you want to understand financial statement analysis **the easy way—without wasting months on confusing textbooks**? If yes, you've found the right book.

Most books on this subject are either too expensive, too technical, or simply overwhelming. This one is different. Written by a university instructor with over ten years of teaching experience, it takes the most complex ideas and explains them in **clear, practical, everyday language**—so you can learn faster and with confidence.

This book was crafted over the course of a year with one mission: to deliver **top-quality financial education at the lowest possible cost**. It's not just another theory-heavy manual—it's a **step-by-step guide** that you can finish in just one week. And with free video lectures available on YouTube and Dailymotion, your learning doesn't stop at the book— you'll have a complete learning package at your fingertips.

We believe in **simplicity, speed, and results**. By the time you finish, you won't just "know" financial statement analysis—you'll be able to **apply it immediately** in exams, in business, or in your career.

This is just the beginning. We're committed to bringing you more affordable, high-impact resources in the future. Your feedback and suggestions will help us make each book even better.

So, let's get started. The journey to mastering financial statement analysis begins here.

Regards

Dr. M. Imran Ahsan Dhothar
Ch.imranahsen@gmail.com

Table of Contents

Chapter 1: Introduction to Financial Statement Analysis

Financial statements and their role

Financial reporting: These are the methods used by a firm/company to explain its financial position and financial health. The management prepares unaudited and audited financial statements for the general public and the users of financial statements. The financial statements include income statements, balance sheets, statement of cash flow, and other financial disclosures required by regulatory bodies/accounting standard-setting bodies.

The users of financial statements are those who make economic decisions based on these reports, like investors, Lenders, company management, Government, analysts, etc.

Financial statements analysis is about evaluating a company`s performance by using the published financial reports. The information in the statements and disclosures is used by analysts to evaluate a company`s current and past performance to form an opinion about the firm, such as whether or not we should invest in this company. Or a bank can think of whether or not they should pass the loan application of this particular company.

Different financial statements and their role in evaluating a company's performance and financial position

Statements of Financial Position: Statement of Financial Position is also called the Balance Sheet. It gives us information about the company's assets and liabilities and owner's equity at a particular date.

The balance sheet is very useful as it gives us the information about resources owned by the company (assets) and how the company has financed those resources (liabilities and shareholders' equity). Analysts use this information to evaluate the company.

Assets – liabilities = residual claim in the company by owners.

Statement of comprehensive income: Statement of comprehensive income shows all changes in equity except for shareholders' transactions. Depending on local regulations, it may be combined into two parts (or reported separately)
- The income statement.
- The statement of other comprehensive income.

The income statement: It shows the revenues and expenses from ordinary business operations.

Revenues are inflows from selling goods and or services from normal business activities.

Expenses are outflows (from purchasing raw material and services, etc.) from producing those goods and services.

Other comprehensive income: It generally shows the revenues and expenses from the unusual events and from the items that do not come into the normal course of business operations, like actuarial gains/losses due to foreign exchange rate changes, etc.

Statement of changes in equity: We know that Assets – Liabilities = Shareholders' Equity. It is the total residual claims of owners in the company.

Changes in shareholders' equity are the statements that show how the value of shareholders' (owners) has changed over time.

There are three components of equity

Paid in capital: The money received by the company from selling its shares.

Retained earnings: These are the undistributed profits.

Treasury stock: Sometimes companies buy their own stock. It is the total amount given to investors for buying the stock.

Statement of cash flows: One of the most important document a company have. It shows the cash receipts and payments of the company. These cash flows are grouped into three categories;

CFO, Cash flow from operations: The cash inflows and outflows from main business/normal business activities came under this category.

CFI, Cash flow from investing activities: Cash received or paid from the activities like sale/acquisition of fixed assets (property, plant, and equipment, etc.) or investments in other firms, etc.

CFF, Cash flow from financing activities: Cash inflows/outflows from issuing/ retiring of debt or equity securities. It also includes payment of dividends.

Note: We will discuss in detail all the above concepts. The purpose of this section is only to have an overview.

The importance of financial statement notes and supplementary information, including disclosures of accounting policies, methods, and estimates, and management's commentary

There are two major companies' financial disclosures
- Footnotes
- The management's discussion and analysis.

The footnotes: The footnotes to the financial statements help us to understand the company`s position and performance. They give us information about the company`s fiscal year, standards used in preparation of financial statements, accounting assumptions, insight about unique transactions, and about legal proceedings, employees' benefit plans, contingencies and commitments, acquisitions and disposals of businesses and segments of the firm. (We will discuss all of these later).

Management`s commentary: Also known as the management's discussion and analysis (MD&A), management's report, operating and financial review.
This is also a very crucial source of information for an analyst to understand financial reports. One thing to remember here, the MD&A is generally unaudited.
IFRS guidelines suggest having the following information in this section,

Nature of the business, objectives of management, company's past performance, current business environment, and future outlook, the performance measures used, the company's important relationships, resources owned by the company, and risks.

US GAAP requires that the MD&A must include

- Major Events and future uncertainties which will affect liquidity, capital resources, and the main operations of the firm.
- Inflation and off-balance sheet items, obligations like purchase /sale agreements or any other contractual agreement.
- Accounting policies based on management's judgment.

Objective of audits of financial statements, the types of audit reports, and the importance of effective internal controls

Audit: An audit is an inspection of financial statements and supporting documents by an independent body (an auditor or body of auditors).

Objective of audit: The objective of an audit is to create an opinion about the fairness and reliability of a set of financial statements and documents.

The independent auditor(s) are employed by the board of directors of a company. The auditor is to check whether or not accounting standards have been followed. They also check the company's internal control system, confirm assets and liabilities, and determine whether any material errors exist in the financial statements.

The auditor's examination produces an auditor's report, which has three parts.

- A statement that the auditor has performed an independent review.

- A statement that generally accepted auditing standards were followed and there is a reasonable assurance that the financial documents have no material errors.
- A statement that the auditor is satisfied with the chosen and following accounting standard. Reasonable estimates and assumptions, along with proper accounting policies, were chosen.

Types of report: Auditor's opinion can be one of the following three (also called the three types of report)

Unqualified opinion/report: This is the most common type of report. It is also called a clean report. It suggests that (according to the auditor's view) the financial documents are free of any material errors or omissions, and financial statements have been prepared by following the accounting standards.

Qualified opinion/report: It suggests that some exceptions have been made to the accounting principles in preparation of financial statements. The auditor explains these exceptions in his report.

Adverse opinion: If the auditor finds faults in financial statements, such as the statements not conforming to accounting principles or not being presented fairly, he issues an adverse opinion/report. An adverse opinion is also issued in case the auditor is unable to give an opinion due to a limited scope or the non-availability of proper documents. The adverse report tells us these reports are not reliable at all.

Effective internal controls

Internal control is the process by which a firm tries to ensure the fair and accurate presentation of its financial statements.

Internal control is the responsibility of management. They should keep checking the balances so the auditor can validate them. In the USA, for a publicly traded company, the auditor must express his/her opinion about internal control, either in a separate auditor's report or in the auditor's report.

Information sources that analysts use in financial statement analysis besides annual financial statements and supplementary information.

We know that the companies are required to issue annual reports to show their financial results and performances. But in the meantime, companies also release quarterly and semi-annual reports, which analysts must consider while evaluating the performance of the company. These interim reports (generally unaudited) and their footnotes are a vital source of information to an analyst. These statements show major financial events during that interim.

Other important sources of information are Securities and Exchange Commission filings, like,

Form 8-K: Under Form 8-K, the companies are required to disclose

- Acquisitions and disposals of major assets
- Changes in management or corporate governance.

This form is submitted when changes occur, so this is a very important one.

 Quarterly financial statements are filed under **Form 10-Q.** This also includes any material changes in business and any new information regarding the company's management.

Form 10-K: It is filed with audited annual reports, information about the business, management, and legal matters.

Proxy statements: When there are matters that require shareholders' votes, this statement is issued to them. These are matters like the election of the board of directors, their compensation, etc.

Sources of information other than SEC filings;

Press releases and corporate reports: Companies often release these items. They can be a source of information up to some extent.

Conference calls: This is another important source for an analyst. After earnings are announced, senior management answers the questions in the conference call.

Earnings guidance is given by the management to present its own performance expectations.

Industry reports: the reports of the industry and especially the competitors are also a good source of information.

Analysts must also consider the economic conditions of businesses and the country in analyzing the companies. He/she can get more information from economic and business journals, statistical journals, and govt. journals.

Steps in the financial statement analysis framework

The following is a six-step basic framework for any of the above motivations, also called the six steps in the financial analysis framework.

1. Articulate the purpose and the context of the analysis
2. Collect data
3. Process the data
4. Analyze and interpret the data
5. Develop reports and communicate the conclusions
6. Follow up/update the analysis

1. **Articulate the purpose and the context of the analysis:**
    First of all, we need to articulate what is the purpose of our analysis. An analyst might be working on different perspectives to evaluate a company. These perspectives might include
    Evaluation of a company as an equity investment, Potential acquisition, analysis of the company`s creditworthiness, or any other intentions given by the client.

2. **Collect data:** At this stage, all the sources of information, like financial statements, management`s commentary, conference calls, etc., are needed to collect the data about a company.

3. **Process the data:** At this stage, all the data collected in the previous stage is processed. We might be calculating financial ratios and common size statements, building models, or forecasting, etc.

4. **Analyze and interpret the data:** At this stage, we start to build an assessment about the company. We answer the questions we were looking for in the first stage.

5. **Develop reports and communicate the conclusions:** At this stage, we draw conclusions, develop a report, and

communicate it with the intended audience/client. Report must comply with Codes and Standards.

6. Follow up/update the analysis: At this stage, we gather and update our previously collected data/information and update our conclusions. Updating might include repetition of some previous steps.

Chapter 2: Financial Reporting Standards

Objective of the financial statements and the importance of financial reporting standards in security analysis and valuation

Objective of financial statements

According to the IASB Conceptual Framework for Financial Reporting 2010, the objective of financial statements is to provide useful information about the company to current and potential Investors, Creditors, and Lenders to help them in decision-making about lending or investment in the company.

Importance

These standards ensure

Consistency: it means that these statements should be using consistent methods of calculations and presentation. Similar items must be treated in a similar way.

Comparability: The financial statements should be comparable. Although they are not one hundred percent the same, they should be in a format that helps comparison.

Roles and desirable attributes of financial reporting standards-setting bodies and regulatory authorities in establishing and enforcing reporting standards, and describe the role of international organizations of securities commissions

Standard-setting bodies set the financial reporting standards. Regulatory bodies enforce them.

Standard-setting bodies:

These are independent not for profit organizations. These bodies consist of professional accountants and auditors. There are two major standard-setting bodies: FASB (Federal

Accounting Standards Board) in the US, which established US GAAP (Generally Accepted Accounting Principles), and IASB (International Accounting Standards Board), which sets forth IFRS (International Financial Reporting Standards) for the rest of the world.

Many countries have their own standard-setting bodies, too. FASB and other bodies are working towards convergence with IFRS.

Desirable qualities and attributes of these bodies
- Sufficient resources, capability, and authority
- Clear and consistent standard-setting process
- Independent, but connected to the stakeholders.
- Driven to act in the general public interest. (not self-interest)

Regulatory authorities:
Regulatory authorities enforce the standards set by standard-setting bodies. SEC (Securities and Exchange Commission in the US and FCA (Financial Conduct Authority) in the UK are some examples.

Most of these work for IOSCO (International Organization of Securities Commissions). It is an organization to guide those who regulate local markets. Its members regulate 90 percent of the financial markets.

IOSCO has three objectives:

1. Protect investors,
2. Ensure the market is efficient, fair, and transparent
3. Reduced systematic risk

The following are some filings for public limited companies, required by the SEC (Securities and Exchange Commission, a regulatory authority). These are a very important source of information for an analyst.

Form S-1 Registration statement: It is filed prior to the issuance of new securities. It contains details about the issuer, the underwriter, the risk associated with the security, and disclosure about the usage of funds.

10-K annual filing: It is an annual filing that contains statements about the business and audited financial statements. It also contains legal matters about the company. Equivalent to 10-K SEC forms for foreign issuers in the U.S. markets are Form 40-F and Form 20-F for Canadian companies and other foreign issuers, respectively.

10Q Quarterly filing: It is filed quarterly. It contains any material changes in business and unaudited updates to the financial statements.

DEF-14 A Proxy statement: It is a statement to the SEC that contains matters about shareholders' votes.

8K major material event: This form contains major changes in asset acquisition or disposal. These are the changes in corporate governance, management, or any other accounting policy changes. It is filed whenever the changes occur. So, it's very important for an analyst.

144 Issuance of qualified buyers: In some cases, a company may issue securities to a group of qualified buyers. The company may not have to register securities with the SEC, but they are still required to notify the SEC with Form 144 about this intention.

Forms 3, 4, and 5: These contain beneficial ownership of securities by a company's directors and officers. Analysts can get information from these forms to know about purchases and sales of securities within the company.

Status of global convergence of accounting standards and ongoing barriers to developing one universally accepted set of financial reporting standards.

Status of global convergence: Reasonable efforts have been made to comply with IFRS. In Europe, companies are required to comply with IFRS. In the US, if a company complies with IFRS, the SEC does not require it to comply with US GAAP. Globally, regulatory authorities are making efforts to align with IFRS.

Ongoing barriers:

- The standards-setting bodies and regulatory authorities disagree on the treatment of certain items.
- There is much cost involved in changes in standards and their implications on existing standards.
- There is much political pressure from business cartels/business groups on local regulatory authorities if they change the standards.

International Accounting Standards Board's conceptual framework, including the objective and qualitative characteristics of financial statements, required reporting elements, and constraints and assumptions in preparing financial statements

The objective of the IASB framework is to provide useful financial information to those who are providing resources to the company (i.e., investors, creditors)

The framework outlines the qualitative characteristics, specifies required financial statement elements, and provides various assumptions and constraints in preparation of financial reports to make financial statements useful.

Qualitative characteristics

There are two basic qualitative characteristics that make financial statements useful.

1. Relevance: Information is relevant if it is predictive and confirmatory. It means information in financial statements must help the user (with reasonable accounting/financial knowledge) to predict the future and confirm the current state of the company. It also means the materiality of information.

2. Faithful presentation: It means the information is complete, neutral, and free of error.

The framework also provides us with four more characteristics that ensure relevance and faithful presentation.

i.   **Comparability:** It means the financial statements must be in a format so they can be easily comparable. The presentation must be consistent among entities and periods.

ii.   **Verifiability:** It means that the experts should be able to get the same information by using the same methods.

iii. **Timeliness:** It means the information is provided before the decision maker needs to make decisions.

iv.   **Understandability:** It means that those who have a reasonable understanding of accounting and those who have made reasonable efforts should be able to understand that information.

Required reporting elements

The framework provides us with five groups of required reporting elements. From which three groups measure financial position, while two measure financial performance.

Financial position measuring elements are:

- Assets: The resources owned by the company.
- Liabilities: The obligations of a company.
- Equity: The residual interest of owners in the company. This is what is left after deducting the liabilities from the assets.

Financial performance elements are:

- Incomes: Inflows from the normal business or gains from extraordinary events (not from owner`s contribution).
- Expenses: Outflows from the normal course of business and losses from extraordinary events.

Recognition and measurement of the elements in the accounts

Recognition: It means that an item needs to be recognized if it has probable inflow or outflow, and its cost could be reliably measured.

Measurement: The amount at which the elements are reported depends on the measurement base. There are six possibilities that can be used to measure the value.

i.   <u>Historical cost:</u> The amount originally paid to purchase an asset.

ii.   <u>Amortized cost:</u> Historical cost minus accumulated depreciation.

iii.   <u>Current cost:</u> The amount that can be used to buy an equivalent asset at today's market value.

iv.   <u>Settlement value:</u> It means the amount an asset could be sold for or the amount needed to satisfy a liability.

v.   <u>Present value:</u> A discounted value of future expected cash flows from that item.

vi.   <u>Fair value:</u> The amount that would be exchanged between knowledgeable parties in an arm's length transaction (easily and quickly).

Constraints and assumptions for the preparation of financial statements

Constraints: The framework provides us with two major constraints in the preparation of financial statements, which can be useful.

i.   <u>Cost vs Benefit:</u> The cost of presenting information should be less than the benefits gained from using it.

ii.   <u>Non-quantifiable information:</u> There is some important information which are highly important for the company's future profitability, but it cannot be presented in financial statements because it is not <u>quantifiable</u>. For example, customer loyalty, employee loyalty, and the environment. They must be considered in company analysis.

Assumptions: There are two assumptions that the framework provides us with

<u>Accrual accounting:</u> It means that the economic transaction must be presented in the period in which they occur, not necessarily with cash payment.

i.   <u>Going concern:</u> It means the company is expected to continue in existence for the foreseeable future. As we can imagine, we may have entirely different opinions about the value of the company if it is going to close next year.

General requirements of financial statements under international financial reporting standards (IFRS)

IAS1 (International Accounting Standard 1) tells us which financial statements are required and how they must be presented.

Required statements:

If a company wants to comply with IAS1, it must provide a Balance sheet, Statement of comprehensive income, Cash flow statement, Statement of owner`s equity, and a set of notes (containing an explanation of the accounting policies and significant events necessary to fully understand the statements).

General features:

According to IAS 1, financial statements must have the following features

a.   **Fair presentation:** The statements must present the transactions or events faithfully by following the criteria set out in the framework.

b.   **Going concern:** the IAS 1 tells us to present the financial statement with an assumption of going concern (that the company is not going to be liquidated in the near future).

c. **Accrual accounting:** The accrual accounting principle must be followed in the preparation of financial statements.
d. **Consistency:** The information presented should be consistent between periods. The items should not change significantly from period to period without a significant change in business.
e. **Materiality:** It means that the item that could influence a decision using these statements must not be omitted.
f. **Aggregation:** Similar items should be presented together, and dissimilar items must be reported separately.
g. **No offsetting:** The statements must clearly present assets and liabilities as well as income and expenditures in full. If not specifically guided by IFRS, they must not be offset.
h. **Frequency:** Financial statements must be released at least annually.
i. **Comparative information:** Information from the prior period must be provided along with the current material so they can be compared.

Required structure/ contents:

There are three distinct required contents.

The balance sheet must be classified as current and not current items (assets and liabilities).

There are some elements that the IFRS requires minimum information about, which must be included. For example, the balance sheet must include cash and cash equivalents, plant, property, and equipment, and inventories. The comprehensive income statement must include revenues, profit or loss, tax expense, and finance costs (among other items).

The statements must provide comparative information for all items from prior periods unless there is another IAS rule that contradicts this rule.

Comparison of the key concepts of financial reporting standards under IFRS and the US generally accepted accounting principles (US GAAP) reporting systems.

US GAAP and IFRS differ in the form of Performance elements, recognition of assets, and upward valuation of assets.

The performance elements:

IFSR has only two elements listed as performance elements: Income & Expenses

IFRS defines assets as <u>resources from which future economic benefit is expected.</u>

US GAAP has four performance elements: Revenues, Expenses, Gains and losses, and Comprehensive income

Under GAAP, Assets are defined as future economic benefits.

The measurements and evaluation are the same in both. The IFRS allows upward valuation of assets, but GAAP does not allow it in most cases. GAAP allows the upward evaluation in case of some assets that need to be held at fair value.

Note: Upward valuation will be discussed later in this book in detail

Characteristics of a coherent financial reporting framework and the barriers to creating such a framework

A coherent framework must fulfill the following three characteristics;

1.   **Transparency:** The statements must reflect the underlying business activity more clearly (fair and full disclosure).

2.　　**Comprehensiveness:** No important transaction should be omitted. The statements must completely cover all the financial transactions affecting the business.

3.　　**Consistency:** Similar transactions must be treated in a similar way, allowing comparison across industries and periods.

Barriers to creating a coherent financial reporting framework

There are some conflicts that exist in certain areas in achieving these characteristics called **barriers,** which are,

1. Valuation: There are various methods to value assets and liabilities. For example, historical cost, amortized cost, etc. Sometimes we need subjective judgment to use the appropriate method. And many times, the choices of methods changed from firm to firm.

2. Standard setting: US GAAP is known as a rules-based approach to standard setting, where IFRS is known as a principle-based approach. Different parties with different agendas have different and opposing opinions on the validity of these approaches.

3. Measurement: The balance sheet and income statement are interrelated. But the balance sheet is reported at a single point of time, while the income statement is presented as performance over a period of time. The standard setters mostly set preference on focusing on the balance sheet. Others may rely more on the income/ expense approach (i.e., Income statement).

Implications for financial analysis of differing financial reporting systems and the importance of monitoring developments in financial reporting standards

As the Accounting standards are continuously evolving, an analyst must remain updated about these changes and innovations. Analysts must visit professional journals, the IASB website (www.ifrs.org), and the FASB website (*www.fasb.org*).

An analyst must also check for the company`s disclosures for accounting standards used, accounting policies, and estimates.

Analysis of the company's disclosures of significant accounting policies

Accounting assumptions and policies used by the company must be disclosed in the footnotes of the financial statements. Anything regarding the subjective management decisions must be reported in the Management discussion& analysis.

There are two types of accounting policy disclosures.

1. **Accounting policies disclosure:** These disclosures are a source of extra information about the contents of financial statements.

2. **Changes to accounting policies:** This disclosure is also a vital source of information. This helps us to judge the management team itself and the expected outcomes of these changes in the future.

Chapter 3: Understanding Income Statement

Components of the income statement and alternative presentation formats of that statement

The income statement is known under many names, like
- The income statement.
- The statement of operations.
- The statement of earnings.
- The profit and loss statement.

Whatever the name is, it tells us about the revenues and costs of the company in one financial year.

Components of the income statement

We know that
Net income =Revenue - expenses
Revenue is the company's income from the normal course of business, i.e., from its everyday activities.
Net revenue is revenue that has been adjusted for discounts or potential returns (discount on sales or sales returns).
Expenses: The costs incurred while generating revenues. We have the cost of raw material, labor cost, rent, etc.
Gains and losses: The incomes and costs that are not associated with ordinary business activities. For example, if a company sells its plant and gets some gain (profit) or loss.

Revenues + other sources of income + extraordinary gains - ordinary business expenses - other expenses - extraordinary losses = **net income**

Alternative presentations

Different companies present income statement items differently

For example, some companies put current-year items on the left and others on the right.

Some companies use brackets or parentheses when reporting an item that reduces income (i.e., expenses). Other companies use a negative sign. Companies often choose to aggregate certain items together in the report. Selling general and administration expenses, for example, some companies report this as a single line item while others report them separately.

Companies aggregate the items according to the following

Grouping by nature: Grouping by nature means that anything that is basically the same should be listed on the same line, for example, and all kinds of depreciation (depreciation of all long-term assets) would all be grouped together as one item on the report.

Grouping by function: In this method, revenues or expenses are grouped because they have a certain link. For example, in cost of goods sold, we have a bunch of different expenses which are related to the cost of sold goods (i.e., raw material, labor wages, etc.)

Single step VS multistep presentation

This is another difference in the presentation of the income statement. In a single step format, companies put all revenues together and all expenses together. They do not report gross profit or gross loss. Gross profit or losses are presented in a multi-step format.

Remember, revenues do not depend upon cash. When goods are sold on credit, revenue is recognized when
- Ownership of the goods changes hands from the selling to the buying party.
  - o When the risk and reward of owning goods have moved to the buying party.

With IFRS, we must recognize revenues in the sale of goods under the following conditions.
- When the risk and reward of owning goods have moved to the buying party.
- Selling party has no managerial influence/control over the goods.
- The expected revenue can be reliably measured.
- It is likely and probable that the economic benefit of the transaction will flow to the selling entity.
- The cost of the transaction can be reliably measured.

In case of the delivery of services following conditions are followed
- The expected revenue can be reliably measured.
- It is likely and probable that the economic benefits of transactions will flow to the selling party.
- Cost of the transaction can be measured.
- The stage of completion of the transaction must be reliably measured.

With GAAP, revenue must be recognized if it is Realized, realizable or earned.

These are some special cases in which revenue recognition becomes more difficult.
Special cases can be
- long-term contracts
- Installment sales.
- Barter transactions.
- The gross and net reporting of revenue.

Long-term contracts: Long-term contracts mean revenue streams will cover multiple accounting periods (more than one year).

The issue is when we recognize the revenue. If we recognize it when the contract occurred, that will exaggerate reported income in the current period, and the income for subsequent years will be underweight.

So, we need to divide the overall revenue amount across multiple years, maybe an equal are prorated(unequal) distribution across each year or maybe recognition should be based on our understanding of the underlying business circumstances using a method called

i.   *Percentage of completion.*

It estimates what percentage of the contract is complete. If the contract is 60 % complete, then 60 % of the revenue should be recognized by the company up to that point. We calculate the percentage of completion of a project by calculating the percentage of the total cost we have spent.

For example, a company has entered into a project which will take five years to complete.

Total cost of the project is estimated = $20 million

Price at which it will be sold =$30 m.

In the first year, we spent 5million, which is 25 percent of the overall cost.

So, 25% of total revenues (25% of 30 m) should be reported for the first year and the same method for the next years.

ii. *If the outcome of the project is not actually known at the beginning of a long-term contract.*

IFRS and U. S. GAAP differ in this circumstance.

Under IFRS as long as we have sufficient incoming revenue to justify the level of spending we can recognize revenue to the extent of the costs incurred. It means revenues =costs. Profit is only recognized at completion.

Under US GAAP, we use the completed contract method. The project doesn't go to the income statement at all. Only loss is recognized immediately. The cumulative cost is recorded on the balance sheet, where cash is going down as it is spent. And some other asset (inventory) is rising as the project is on its way to completion. In the final year, we record total revenue and total cost. In years other than the final, we do not recognize any costs or revenues under US GAAP.

Installment sales (Another long-term contract)

This is a situation where sales proceeds are to be received in installments over multiple periods.

Under IFRS, the expected installment payments are discounted back to their present value. That discounted amount is then recognized on the date of the sale as the sales price. The remainder, the difference between the simple sum of payments and the present value of those payments, will be recognized over time as an interest component.

Under U.S GAAP, we have two methods
- Installment method
- Cost recovery method

Let's understand these two with the help of an example.

Let's say a company is selling one of its plants.

The cost of the plant was $5m and they have agreed a price of $8m. The buying party has offered a down payment of $1.5m, and the remaining $6.5 m will be paid over a period of 10 years.

Under the installment method, a portion of profit is recognized in line with the percentage of the total sales price that is profit.

In our case the total profit is $3 m, which is 37.5 % of total deal value ($8m**)**

Then we take 37.5 % of the down payment (1.5 m) to get a profit attributable to the down payment of $562500.

And whenever we receive cash, 37.5 percent will be recognized as profit, and the remaining is cost.

Cost recovery method: In this method profit cannot be recorded until the amount of cash is greater than the initial cost so because the cash amount paid by the buyer is not higher than the original cost no profit would be recorded unless when the cash amount exceeds the cost it will be recorded as profit in coming periods.

Barter transactions:

Let's say two companies are exchanging advertising space. It means they are exchanging very similar assets or services to each other.

So, there should be very little or no effect on income.

Under IFRS, revenue can be recognized from this type of transaction in an amount equal to that from a similar non-barter transaction between unrelated parties.

Under US GAAP, we can only recognize revenue from barter transactions if we have previously recognized cash for a similar transaction.

Revenue Recognition Steps

There are five steps involved in recognizing revenue:

1. Identify the contract (or contracts) pertaining to a customer
2. Identify performance obligations in the contract
3. Determine the transaction price (or prices)
4. Allocate the transaction price (or prices) to the performance obligations in each contract
5. Recognize revenue whenever the entity satisfies a performance obligation.

Calculations of revenues and other information that might influence the choice of revenue recognition method

Normally, firms buy products and or raw materials from their suppliers and sell to their customers. So, cost of goods sold and revenues are easily distinguishable.

With e-business, companies were selling products that they never purchased or manufactured. They simply take in the revenue and then arrange delivery to the customer directly from the supplier.

The question is should they be reporting revenue in the full amount received from the customer (called gross revenue reporting) or their earnings only (called net revenues reporting) since earnings are more like a commission as the spread between the amount they have received in the cost of them from the supplier.

Under U. S. GAAP: If the following conditions are fulfilled, the firm can report gross revenues; otherwise, net revenues.
- If the selling company is the primary under a contract.
- If they bear inventory risk and credit risk.
- If they have more than one supplier.

- They have reasonable influence over the price.

General principles of expense recognition, specific expense recognition applications, and implications of expense recognition choices for financial analysis

Expenses: The IASB Conceptual Framework describes expenses as "decreases in economic benefits during the accounting period in the form of outflows or depletions of assets or increases in liabilities that result in decreases in equity, other than those relating to distributions to equity participants."

General Principles of Expense Recognition: A company recognizes expenses in the period that it consumes the economic benefits associated with the expenditure or loses some previously recognized economic benefit.

Matching principle: Under the matching principle, a company recognizes some expenses (for example, cost of goods sold) whenever the associated revenues are recognized.

Matching requires that a company recognizes the cost of goods sold in the same period as revenues from the sale of the goods. **Matching is applied to inventory and cost of goods sold**.

Period costs are expenditures that do not directly match revenue and are reflected in the period when a company incurs a liability or has an expenditure. For example, administrative expenses.

Specific identification method, the inventory and cost of goods sold are based on their physical flow. IFRS and US GAAP, however, permit the use of the first-in, first-out (FIFO) method and the weighted average cost method to assign costs.

FIFO method: In this method, the oldest goods that are purchased /manufactured are sold first, while the newest goods purchased or manufactured remain in inventory. So, the ending inventory would include the most recent purchases.

Weighted average cost method: In this method, the average costs of goods available for sale are assigned to the units sold and the units remaining in inventory.

Last in, first out (LIFO) method: This method is only allowed under US GAAP, but IFRS does not permit it. Under this method, the newest goods that are purchased /manufactured are sold first, while the oldest goods purchased/manufactured remain in inventory. So, the costs of the newest items purchased will flow into the costs of goods sold first.

Specific Expense Recognition Applications
Doubtful accounts: While using the matching principle, once revenue is recognized, a company is required to record an estimate of uncollectible revenues. This estimate is recorded as uncollectable reserve/ reserve for doubtable debts (an expense) on the income statement, not deducted from revenues directly.

Warranties: While recognizing revenues from sales of warrantable goods and or services, companies are required to estimate the amount of future expenses that might result from these warranties, to recognize estimated warranty expenses in the period of sale (not in a later date).

Depreciation and Amortization: Depreciation is the process of systematically allocating the costs of long-lived assets over their useful life. There are many methods for computing depreciation. These are the straight-line method, the diminishing balance method, and the units of production method.

Straight-line method: Under this method cost of long-lived assets less the estimated residual value is allocated evenly over the estimated useful life of the asset.

Annual Depreciation under straight line method =
$$\frac{Cost - residual\ value}{Useful\ life}$$

Example: ABS Company purchases machinery at a cost of $10 m. They expect to use it for 10 years, after which they will sell it for $1m. Calculate annual depreciation using the straight line method.

Solution: We know the formula for straight lie method,
Annual Depreciation under straight line method =
$$\frac{Cost - residual\ value}{Useful\ life}$$

By putting values in our formula, we got, annual depreciation = $\frac{10m - 1m}{10}$ =900000$

Diminishing balance method and the units of production methods are referred to as **accelerated methods of**

depreciation because they accelerate the timing of depreciation by allocating a greater proportion of the depreciation expense to the early years of an asset's useful life.

Amortization Expense Recognition

The term amortization is used whenever the long-lived assets are intangible and have a finite, useful life. Amortization expense should match the proportion of the asset's benefits used during the period. Many firms use the straight-line method to calculate annual amortization expense. Straight-line amortization is exactly like straight-line depreciation. Intangible assets with indefinite lives, like goodwill, are not amortized and must be annually tested for impairment. If these items are impaired, the impairment amount is an expense that must be included in the income statement as an expense.

Implications of Expense Recognition Choices for Financial Analysis

The choice of depreciation or amortization method, as well as the estimate of useful life and residual value, can affect a company's reported net income. Also, the estimates that the company uses for doubtful debts and warranty expenses affect net income.

An analyst, having familiarity with the monetary effects of different expense recognition policies and estimates, can efficiently compare different companies or within a single company's historical performance. These effects may be used to adjust for better comparison.

Financial reporting treatment and analysis of non-recurring items (including discontinued operations, unusual or infrequent items) and changes in accounting policies

When evaluating a company's future earnings, it is important to separate incomes and expenses that are likely to continue in the future from those that are less likely to continue.

IFRS and U. S. GAAP do offer some guidelines to separate them, but some items have less clear future and require some judgment from analysts. *We are going to look in*

1. Discontinued operations
2. Extraordinary items.
3. Unusual or infrequent items.
4. Changes in accounting policies
5. Operating versus non-operating items.

A discontinued operation is a part of the business that is being disposed of. It means that part is not going to play any role in the future.

Both US GAAP and IFRS require this to be reported on the income statement separately as a discontinued operation. Since that part of the business will not drive revenue in the future, it is eliminated when developing a forecast.

Extraordinary Items: Items of income and expense that are considered both infrequent and unusual are considered extraordinary.

This classification is not permitted under IFRS. After December 2015, US GAAP also does not permit this classification. But before December 2015, under U. S. GAAP, this classification existed.

Unusual or infrequent items: These are reported before tax with continued operations.

Items that are considered in this category include

- Sale of the business unit at a considerable premium (gains) or discount (losses).
- Gains or losses from Impairments, write-offs, write-downs, restructuring charges.

Under US GAAP items which are either unusual or infrequent are not considered extraordinary you need to be both unusual and infrequent for that classification.

For example, restructuring charges or the sale of the business unit at a considerable premium or discount. These items will be reported with the company's continuing operations.

Under IFRS, the accounting treatment is a bit different. Based on the idea that a single income or expense that is material or relevant to the understanding of the business should be reported separately, anything unusual or infrequent would have to be reported separately.

Changes in accounting policies:

The change in accounting policy could be of two types.

- A new accounting standard set up by the standard-setting authority or company decided to move from IFRS to GAAP or vice versa.
- Changes in accounting estimates

Changes in applicable accounting standards are required to be applied retrospectively. It means whenever a company changes its accounting standard, they are required to restate its previous financial statements according to the new standards because it would be misleading for a company to be able to use two different sets of accounting standards on the same document side by side. (Use of LIFO is an exception here. We will discuss it under inventories in detail.)

Change in an accounting estimate: The effect of a change in an accounting estimate is not required to be applied retrospectively. Because it depends upon the management`s judgment, usually after getting new information.

For example, if the management realizes that some specific asset has a longer or shorter useful life than previously estimated. It will significantly change expense (depreciation), and it is required to be mentioned in the notes accompanying the statement.

Analytical implications:

In forecasting, there is considerable judgment at the end of the analyst that is needed. The analyst has to decide whether he should include any item or remove it from the analysis. Analysts must see whether or not new policies have an effect on cash flow. If they have, more care is required at the end of the analysis to include or exclude items from the analysis. Changes in standards are disclosed, and the documents are restated according to new standards, so there is not much to worry about in this case.

Distinguish between the operating and non-operating components of the income statement.

Operating and Non-operating items

First of all, we need to understand the <u>central business activities of the company</u>.

If a company delivers a specific good and or service, all revenues and costs associated with those goods and or services are considered operating items. <u>Any revenue or cost not associated with the company`s central business is more than likely a non-operating item and must be reported separately.</u>

For example, a non-financial services company`s interest on debt and dividends on equity would be more likely to be non-operating items.

On the other hand, financial services companies must classify interest and or dividends as operating items.

So, the activities related to the core business are operating, while other activities are called non-operating activities.

Both IFRS and U. S. GAAP have some specific rules on interest and dividends and where they should be reported in certain circumstances. But as an analyst, the main goal is to understand the reasoning a company has for holding an investment.

Calculations and interpretation of EPS for both simple and complex capital structures

Simple and complex capital structure: If a company issues any financial instruments that can be converted into common stock, then we have a complex capital structure, and if not, it means we have a simple capital structure.

EPS stands for earnings per share, and basic EPS is just that. Basic EPS = company's earnings that are available for distribution to common stockholders / weighted average number of shares of common stock outstanding

Diluted EPS takes a company's complex capital structure into account.

Basic and diluted EPS are the same if the company has a simple capital structure.

Diluted EPS is a performance metric used to gauge the quality of a company's **earnings per share** (**EPS**) if all convertible securities were exercised (converted into common stock). If convertibles exist, they bring down the diluted EPS from basic EPS.

Dilutive and anti-dilutive securities:
Dilutive securities are those that bring up the number of shares outstanding in the calculation of diluted EPS and bring the EPS figure down.
Anti-dilutive securities are those that, if they were converted and included, would bring EPS up.

Converting income statements to common-size income statements and evaluation

Common-size analysis of the income statement:
When building a vertical common-size income statement, every item in the income statement is described as a percentage of revenue. (i.e. $\frac{Cost\ of\ goods\ sold}{Revenues} \times 100$)

By doing this, we eliminate the size effect and standardize the statement to facilitate comparison in terms of its past performance and also in comparison with other companies in the industry.

By combining common-size analysis with profitability ratios, we can come up with some very quick insights into the performance of the company.

Two major components of that analysis are the gross profit margin $(= \frac{Gross\ profit}{Revenues} \times 100)$, and net profit margin Net profit margin$=\frac{Net\ profit}{Revenues} \times 100$.

Gross profit margin is generally an indicator of a company's strategy. Now, a higher GP margin indicates lower costs, which is desirable, but an analyst must analyze why a company is different from its peer group.

Are they using a new technology so their production procedure becomes more efficient than others?

Net profit margin tells us how much money we are earning for every dollar of revenue. There are several components that can be manipulated to get a higher NP. Analysts must consider them. Still lower NP is not desirable.

Let's convert the income statement of ABC Corporation Ltd into common size

Sales	100 m
CGS	-20m
GP	80m
Admin expenses	-1m
Selling expenses	-1m
Net profit	78m

Common-size income statement

Sales	00/100) x100 =100%
CGS	20/100) x100 =20%
GP	80%
Admin expenses	1%
Selling expenses	1%
Net profit	78%

Comprehensive income

Under IFRS, total comprehensive income is defined as the change in equity during the period resulting from transactions and other events other than those resulting from transactions with owners in their capacity as owners.

Under US GAAP total comprehensive income is defined as the change in equity, net assets on the business enterprise during the period from transactions and other events and circumstances from non-owner sources.

We know that Net income revenues – expenses incurred in the generation of those revenues.

But total comprehensive income is bigger than net income. It includes all changes in equity during a period except contributions by owners and distributions to owners. So

Total comprehensive = net income + other comprehensive income (non-reported items).

Other comprehensive income:

There are four major transactions that are included in other comprehensive income and not in net income.

- Gains and losses from foreign currency exchange.
- Adjustments to the minimum pension liability.
- Any unrealized gains or losses from cash flow hedging derivatives.
- Unrealized gains and losses from available-for-sale securities.

If reporting under IFRS, the company may choose to hold an asset in its books at fair value rather than depreciating it from historical cost.

Revaluations in this regard would also be included in other comprehensive income.

Chapter 4: Understanding Balance Sheets

Elements of the balance sheet: Assets, liabilities and equity

A balance sheet is also known as the statement of financial position or the statement of financial condition.

It shows the financial situation of a company at a single point in time. It shows what a company owns, owes, and what the owners' claims are on that company.

There are three basic elements of a balance sheet

Assets, liabilities and equity.

Assets: Resources owned by the company for future economic benefits. These resources are a result of past transactions or events. These resources are expected to make inflows for the company.

Liabilities: Obligations on a company resulted from past transactions or events. These are expected to make an outflow from the company.

Equity: This is residual claims of owners in a company. Equity = Assets − Liabilities. Equity is also called owner`s equity or shareholders' equity. Sometimes it is also called net assets.

To make a balance sheet, we need to follow basic balance sheet equation

**Assets = Liabilities + Equity.**

It means assets, which are resources owned by the company, are either financed by creating liabilities or by owner`s equity.

Uses and limitations of the balance sheet in financial analysis

A balance sheet shows the financial position of a company at a single point in time in terms of what the company owns, owes, and what claims the owners have. It shows the financial health of the company.

With the help of a balance sheet, we can determine the company`s liquidity position, solvency position, and its ability to distribute cash to the owners. Liquidity means a firm`s ability to meet short-term obligations. Solvency means a firm`s ability to meet long-term obligations.

Limitations of balance sheet: A company`s balance sheet does not necessarily reflect its intrinsic market value because of three major reasons.

1.   Mixed valuation methods. Assets and liabilities are measured using different methods of valuation. Some reported on historical cost, some on fair value, and the overall picture shows the judgment of the management, which is not necessarily a reflection of how the market values them.

2.   Single point in time: The balance sheet is reported at a single point in time. It means even the stated value of assets will only be accurate if the report is released when those valuations apply. After some time, they may be out of dated.

3. Other factors: There are significant numbers of factors that affect the company's value and not all of them are considered and shown on the balance sheet. For example, customer and employee loyalty leads to good relations with suppliers, etc.

Alternative formats of balance sheet presentation.

There are two styles for balance sheet presentation,
1.   Classified style
2.   Liquidity-based style

IFRS and US GAAP allow classified style, but the liquidity-based style is only permitted under IFRS.

Classified style: In this style, a company's accounts are separated into current and non-current assets and current and non-current liabilities.

Liquidity-based style: In this method, we present the accounts in order of liquidity. We still have the distinction between assets, liabilities and equity but (rather than classifying items in terms of their current or non-current nature) we order all accounts under their broader categories in terms of liquidity. This style is more often used in banking.

Distinguish between current and non-current assets and current and non-current liabilities

Current assets: An item is current asset if it fulfills any of the following conditions
- An instrument held for trading.
- An item that is expected to be sold in either a year or one operating cycle whichever is longer.
- An item that is expected to be used in either a year or one operating cycle whichever is longer. Or
- An item that is somehow expected to be converted into cash in either a year or one operating cycle, whichever is longer.

Current assets are usually listed in the balance sheet according to their liquidity. More liquids are at first position like cash. Current assets reveal the operating activities of a firm.

Operating cycle: It is the time period from the purchase of goods or materials through the sale of the product and the collection of cash.

Non-current assets: These are assets that are not quickly convertible into cash or used within one operating cycle (do not fulfill the conditions of current assets).

These assets provide information about the company's investing activities.

Current liabilities: If any one of the following definitions for a liability is fulfilled, we call it a current liability.
- Liabilities held for trading,
- A liability expected to settle within a year or a single operating cycle is current
- For a liability to be current, the company must not have the unconditional right to push it into next period.

Non-current liabilities:

For a liability, if any of the above-mentioned characteristics are not fulfilled, then we have a non-current liability. These are longer-term obligations and reveal the firm's investing activities.

Different types of assets and liabilities, and the measurement bases of each.

Part 1: Assets.

Current assets: These are the assets that will be used in one operating cycle or within one year, whichever is longer. Some common current assets are

Cash and cash equivalents: These are the most liquid current assets. It is places at top in current assets. Under cash and cash equivalents, we have a cash balance held at banks and short-term instruments like a U. S. treasury bill, which can be easily and quickly converted into cash and have minimal interest rate risk. These are held at fair value or at amortized cost. These are considered financial assets.

Marketable securities: It means Investments with a little more risk than cash equivalents. Normally, in this section, we have publicly traded debt and equity securities like government securities, notes, bonds, etc.

Trade receivables: These are the sum of amount due on accounts from customers that arise from sale of goods and or services rendered.

Receivables provide us with useful information about the company's relationship with its customers. Does the company have a diversified group of buyers, or are they concentrated and dependent on a small group? Trade receivables (also called accounts receivable) are held at net realizable value. Net realizable value = gross receivables − provision for bad debts. The amount of bad debts provision must be closer to industry norms. Because the management can undervalue this provision to overstate the earnings.

Inventory: Raw material, work in process, and finished products come in this category. It is important to note that not every company has things like this in inventory because not every firm manufactures and sells. With inventory analysis we must understand the business of that company.

Certain costs can also be included in the value of inventory, such as purchase price, the cost involved in bringing the inventory to a usable location in a usable condition. Some costs cannot be included in inventory value, like abnormal waste of material or labor, etc., storage costs (if storage is crucial, i.e., for perishable goods, it is included), the administrative overheads, and selling costs.

Under IFRS, inventory must be held in the balance sheet at the lower of cost or net realizable value. Net realizable value = estimated selling price - costs of completion - any costs incurred in making a sale.

Under U. S. GAAP, valuation is based on the lower of cost or market. Market is normally equal to replacement cost. It cannot be greater than net realizable value and also
Market < net realizable value - normal profit margin.
Important: Under IFRS, if the value of inventory is written down and then afterwards the value rises, we can adjust the value of the account upwards.
U. S. GAAP does not allow award reversal of inventory.

Two methods to value inventory: **Standard costing method:** It takes into account materials and labor. This method is used by manufacturing firms and they assign predetermined costs of raw material, labor, and overhead. **Retail method** means using gross margin and sales value to estimate cost.

Continuing with current assets, we have;
Prepayments: Operating expenses that a company has paid in advance. It means we pay an expense in a different period from the period when the expense is actually incurred. We have a cash outflow in one year, but the corresponding expense will show up in the next year. In this case, we create a current asset and write it down as it is used. For example, prepaid insurance, etc.

Deferred tax assets: Two ways to present deferred tax assets.

First, we can bring forward tax assets from periods where we made a net loss to offset the tax bills on periods where we have net profits.

Secondly, we may be required to report a certain amount of income for tax purposes. At the same time, we might have a figure for tax expense which is driven by the amount of income we have chosen to recognize in that period. The actual amount of tax paid is higher than the reported tax expense, which we will be able to carry a deferred tax asset forward into the next period.

Non-current assets

Property, plant, and equipment: Any property intended to be used for administrative purposes or the production of goods or services would be included in plant property and equipment (PP&E). PP&E are tangible assets that are expected to provide economic benefits over multiple periods.

Under IFRS, PP&E is reported using the cost or revaluation model.

U. S. GAAP only allows the cost model.

1. Cost model: This is the carrying value of an asset on the balance sheet, which is the amortized cost of the asset. Amortized cost = historical cost of the asset - accumulated depreciation   -impairment   loss-   depletion   - amortization. **Historical cost** =all costs from purchasing plus the cost involved in getting the asset into working order.

Depreciation is the distribution of an asset's cost over multiple periods. If there is a sudden and unexpected change in value, it might not accurately reflect the value of an asset

To deal with sudden changes in value, there is another concept called **impairment loss.** This account is created to reflect the sudden drop in value when the carrying value of an asset is greater than> asset`s recoverable value.

Recoverable value: An asset`s recoverable amount is the higher of its fair value less cost to sell or its value in use.

It is the amount of cash we can get by selling the asset in an arm's length transaction.

Value in use = present value of expected future cash flows of the asset.

If, after impairment loss, there is recovery, it can be recorded under IFRS, but US GAAP does not allow recovery.

After the cost model, we have the revaluation model.

2.   **Revaluation model:** Property, plant, and equipment is recorded at fair value minus accumulated depreciation. Any change in fair value must affect shareholders' equity. Sometimes, a change in fair value is also recorded in the income statement.

Next in non-current assets, we have
Investment property:
Any property in a company`s possession for investment purposes to gain financial benefits from rental income or capital appreciation is investment property.

IFRS allows us to use either the cost model or the fair value model to report investment property. When using the fair value model, any change in fair value will be reported in the income statement.

U. S. GAAP does not offer specific guidance here.

Intangible assets: Intangible assets are defined as non-monetary assets having no physical existence.

For example, goodwill and trademarks.

IFRS allows us to use either the cost model or the revaluation model, where US GAAP only permits the cost model.

There are two types of intangible assets.

<u>Intangible assets with finite life:</u> We amortize these as normal. It means we systematically allocate the value of the asset to the available years of useful life and also account for unexpected changes in value. (as we did for property, plant, and equipment using impairment)

<u>Intangible assets with indefinite lives:</u> We do not amortize these assets, but we test the value annually and write down in case of impairment. For example, goodwill.

Part two, Liabilities:

Current liabilities:

These are the liabilities which will be satisfied (paid) in one operating cycle or in one year, whichever is longer. The following are the most common current liabilities.

Trade payables: These are the payables of the firm for goods and or services that the company has purchased on credit. There are various ways in which this figure can be interpreted. An increasing tendency in payables might tell us that the firm is taking advantage of the available credit opportunities and reducing the short-term borrowings.

On the other hand, it may reflect that relationships between the supplier and the company are getting worse. An analyst must look for sudden changes, and if that happens, he should investigate further.

Notes payable: It means financial borrowings payable within a year or in an operating cycle. Notes payable may include short-term borrowing from bankers or trade creditors. It also includes the current portion of long-term debt (interest payable).

Accrued liabilities: These are expenses that have been recognized but have not yet been paid. This can include accrued expenses, income tax payable, interest payable, wages payable, and other non-financial liabilities.

Unearned revenue: Revenues the company has taken in but has not earned yet. It means the service has not yet been provided or the goods have not yet been delivered, but an inflow of cash has occurred. For example, advance receipts from customers.

Non-current liabilities:

These are obligations that are not satisfied in one operating cycle or one year. The following are some common non-current liabilities.

Long-term financial liabilities: it means financial obligations that a company owes, are not expected to be settled in one operating cycle or one year. For example, a loan obtained for 5 years or a long-term bond. These must be held in the balance sheet on amortized cost.

Deferred tax liabilities: It is the income tax payable in the future as a result of taxable temporary differences.

Deferred tax liability is created when the tax expense recognized is greater than the tax payable. A very good example for this is when a company chose to use accelerated depreciation for tax purposes but uses the straight line method for financial reporting.

Using the accelerated depreciation method, the depreciation expense will be higher in the first period, and the tax payable will be less. Of course, the tax payable would be higher in later periods. For this company, choose to recognize higher tax payable in the first period, so the effect will be offset in the coming years.

Components of shareholders' equity.

There are six components of owner's equity.
1.   Contributed capital
2.   Preferred stock
3.   Treasury stock
4.   Cumulated other comprehensive income
5.   Non-controlling interests
6.   Retained earnings.

1.   **Contributed capital**: Also known as issued capital. The capital contributed by the owners. The company issues common stock in return for the contributed capital. The number of authorized, issued, and outstanding shares must be disclosed on the company's balance sheet under equity. **Authorized shares** are the number of shares that can be issued under the company`s articles of incorporation. **Issued shares** are the number of shares issued to the public. **Outstanding shares** are the issued shares minus the number of shares the company has purchased back (if any).

2.   **Preferred stock:** Preferred stockholders have higher seniority than common shareholders. When a company is liquidated or issues a dividend, preferred stockholders are paid

first. Preferred stockholders get dividends at a specific rate, usually as a percentage of par value. But they do not have any voting rights.

Preferred stocks can be classified as equity or a financial liability depending on the circumstances. If preferred stock is perpetual and non-redeemable shares (cannot be bought back by the company), then they are classified as equity. If they are redeemable on a fixed date at a certain price, they would be classed as a financial liability. When a company repurchases its own shares, it can hold or cancel them. When they hold shares, those are called **treasury stocks**. The company can resell them in the future if it holds them.

There are the following reasons why a company buys its own stock
1. Management thinks shares are undervalued.
2. Shares are needed to meet employee stock option obligations.
3. The company wants to reduce or offset the dilution effect.

With **cumulative preferred** shares, the company has to pay any missing dividends to preferred stockholders before paying anything to common stockholders. With **participating preferred** stock, the preferred stockholders get additional dividends if the company's profits go beyond a certain level. Preferred stocks can also be converted into common stocks at a predetermined rate.

3. **Treasury stock** is not considered for votes or dividends.

4. **Accumulated other comprehensive income:** The accumulated value of Income Company has earned but not

recognized as part of net income on its income statement because these revenues are not from ordinary business activities. These are changes in stockholders' equity other than net income and owners' contributions, like dividend payments, issuing stock.

5.   **Retained earnings**: The Company`s income that has not been paid out in dividends.

Converting balance sheets to common-size balance sheets and interpretations

Divide the amount of each item on the balance sheet by the amount of total assets and multiply the result by 100. For example, if the cash account is $10,000, divide $10,000 by total assets and then multiply by 100. [$(1000/total\ assets)\ x\ 100]$.

Do the same with other items like inventory, notes payable, PP&E, and bank loans, etc.

Interpreting the common-size balance sheet:
First of all, we should look at the firm`s liquidity position. It means how their current assets are, compared to the current liabilities as a percentage of total assets. The higher the percentage of current assets, the better.

Secondly, we need to analyze the firm's **cash position** compared to current liabilities. Do we have enough cash to meet near-term obligations? If not, then the company will have to pull in some cash from the sale of inventory (which is a bad sign).

Inventory: High levels of inventory percentage show the company is potentially risking obsolescence, and low levels indicate the potential risk of stock shortage. Ideally, these percentages must be close to industry norms or peer groups.

Now let's talk about the company's ability to meet long-term obligations [long-term liabilities/total assets]. What portion of total assets are financed or represented by long-term debt? A higher level of long-term debt as a proportion of total assets indicates that the company is not going to meet long-term obligations and has a risk of insolvency.

Calculations and interpretations of liquidity and solvency ratios

Liquidity-based ratios: Measures a firm's ability to meet short-term obligations. But these ratios must not be considered in isolation. They must be considered collectively.

Current ratio: = current assets / current Liabilities. It measures how many times a firm has current assets to meet current liabilities. A ratio of 1 or higher is desirable. One drawback of the current ratio is that the makeup of current assets could be very different from company to company. So, the current ratio could be very misleading. For example, if a firm has more inventory and less cash, the current ratio might be greater than one, but this situation is not ideal (as inventory is not considered a great source of finance in the short term).

To cover this flaw, we have **the quick ratio, which considers** more liquid assets. Quick ratio = {Cash + marketable securities + receivables} / Current liabilities.

Cash ratio= {cash + marketable securities} / current liabilities.

Solvency ratios:

Long-term debt to equity ratio = the total amount of long-term debt / total equity.

Total debt to total equity ratio = total debt / total equity

Debt ratio = total debt / total assets.

Financial leverage = total assets / total equity.

These ratios show the company's ability to meet long-term obligations. We need to look at trends in these ratios from a company's historical figures to assess the company's performance over time. We can use these ratios to compare with the peer group. But these ratios must also be considered collectively.

Chapter5: Understanding Cash Flow Statements

Cash flows from operating, investing, and financing activities

In this LOS, we need to understand the difference among the three parts of Cash flow. These three parts are
1. **CFO** cash flow from operations.
2. **CFI** cash flow from investing activities.
3. **CFF** cash flow from financing activities.

CFO cash flow from operations: In this heading, we have all cash-based transactions that affect the company's net income. It means day-to-day inflows and outflows related to the company's ordinary business activities.

An example of inflows: Incoming cash received from customers. Proceeds of selling securities held for trading.

Outflows: Cash paid to employees or vendors. Acquisition of the securities, etc.

Under IFRS

Interest received and interest paid can be classified as either operating or financing activities.

With dividends, IFRS offers us the choice between CFO and CFI.

Under US GAAP, Interest and dividends received and interest paid are also classified as operating, but dividends paid are not a component of CFO under U. S. GAAP. U. S. GAAP classifies dividends paid as a financing activity.

CFI cash flow from investing activity: In terms of inflows, Proceeds from the sale of non-trading securities or assets like plant property and equipment or intangible assets.

Outflows: Cash payments to bring these kinds of assets into the firm.

CFF Cash flow from financing: These are Cash flows related to the firm's capital structure.

Inflows may include money received from the issuance of equity, bonds, or cash borrowed.

Outflows: Money used to repurchase common stock. Paying a bond or paying other borrowings.

How non-cash investing and financing activities are reported.

Since there is no cash changing hands in this kind of transaction, it's not going to be recorded in the cash flow statement, but needs to be disclosed either in footnotes to the financials or in a supplementary disclosure.

Cash flow statements prepared under International Financial Reporting Standards (IFRS) and US generally accepted accounting principles (US GAAP)

Under IFRS

Interest received and interest paid can be classified as either operating or financing activities. In terms of dividends, IFRS offers us the choice between CFO and CFI.

Under US GAAP, Interest and dividends received and interest paid are also classified as operating, but dividends paid are not a component of CFO under U. S.

GAAP.U. S. GAAP classifies dividends paid as a financing activity.

Another difference between these two is in the form of income tax paid. Under US GAAP, all taxes paid are reported as operating activities, even if the tax is related to financing or investing activities. Under IFRS, income tax is an operating activity, but if the tax is related to financing or investing activities, it is reported there (not in operating activities).

Direct and indirect methods of presenting cash from operating activities

We have two methods to present a cash flow statement: the direct method and the indirect method.

CFI is the same in these two methods. The choice of method only affects the CFO and CFF.

Direct method: In this method, we take the accrual-based income statement line by line and convert it into a cash-based report. We start from the top of the income statement and go down through line by line.

Example of the direct method

XYX Corporation
Operating cash flow statement – Direct method
For the year ended 31 Dec. 2x18

Cash received from customers*	10000
(less) Cash paid to suppliers	2000
(less) Cash paid for Operating expenses	1000
(less) Cash paid for interest	100
(less) Cash paid for taxes	150
Operating cash flow	6750

*Cash received from customers = sales + Decrease in account receivables - Increase in account receivables

Indirect method: In this method, we start with net income and make adjustments to eliminate non-cash elements of the income statement, like depreciation and amortization, to get operating cash flow.

Let's discuss how do changes in the balance sheet affect cash flow from operations.

There's a direct relationship between how assets/ liabilities change and cash changes.

When an asset`s account increases or a liability account decreases, that indicates that the company is using cash.

On the other hand, when an asset account decreases or a liability account increases, that's cash coming into the company (source of cash).

Example of the indirect method of the cash flow statement

XYX Corporation
Operating cash flow statement-Indirect method
For the year ended 31 Dec. 2x19

Net Income	5000
Add Depreciation expense	100
Add Amortization	100
Less Increase in Accounts Receivable	50
Less increase in inventory	100
Add Decrease in prepaid expenses	2000
Less decrease in accounts payable	250
Less decrease in accrued liabilities	50
Operation cash flow	6750

Reasons for using the direct method or the indirect method

The direct method shows us cash receipts and cash payments separately, whereas the indirect method only shows us the net cash flow, so the direct method provides us with more information.

On the other hand, the indirect method gives us a valuable insight into the relationship between a company's income and its operating cash flow when building cash flow forecasts. So, the indirect method is more helpful to an analyst in terms of forecasting, but the direct method is more informative.

How the cash flow statement is linked to the income statement and the balance sheet

Link between cash flow statement and the balance sheet: Cash is an asset on the balance sheet reported at a specific date. Consecutive balance sheets tell us the cash balances at the beginning and the end of a period. The cash flow statement explains how the change occurred in between.

Relationship between cash flow, the balance sheet, and the income statement: We need to look at individual asset or liability accounts separately. For example, if a company is selling goods, we need to look at how much cash is received and how much goes into receivables. By selling, we get revenues, which come into the income statement. Receivables go into the balance sheet, while cash is in the cash flow statement along with the balance sheet.

Another relationship could be established between changing payables and the cash flow statement, the income statement, and the balance sheet. If the purchases are greater than the cash paid, we know that the payables will increase.

Steps in the preparation of direct and indirect cash flow statements

Remember that regardless of the choice of direct or indirect, CFI and CFF will be the same. Only the CFO is affected by the direct or indirect method.

Direct method: Under this method, net cash flows from operating activities are calculated by taking cash receipts from sales, adding interest and dividends received, and deducting cash payments for purchases, operating expenses, interest, and income taxes.

Cash collections: From accounts receivable, we take the opening receivables plus sales revenues minus the closing balance of receivables, and the resulting amount would be cash collected. In case of unearned revenues, add the opening balances of receivables and unearned revenue, and add the closing balances of receivables and unearned revenue, and proceed as normal.

Cash payments: We need to look at 1. Cash paid to suppliers and 2. Cash paid to employees.

Cash paid to suppliers is just like cash collections. Just look at how the payables accounts change over the period and how much of that change is because the purchase is bigger than the income statement.

Opening payables + purchases - ending balance of payables = cash paid out to suppliers.

If we are not given a purchase figure but given inventory and cost of goods sold, we need to calculate purchases by following the formula

(Ending inventory - Beginning inventory) + Cost of goods sold = Inventory purchases

Cash paid to employees: Look for wages payable changes (balance sheet figure) and wages expense (in the income statement).
Opening balance of wages payable + wages expense (current) - ending balance = cash paid to employees.

Operating expenses: Start with the operating expenses from the income statement. We need to adjust from an accrual basis to a cash basis. An increase in prepayments shows the use of cash. An increase in accrued liabilities indicates a source of cash. It means we have not paid, so we have delayed the outflow.
Cash paid for interest.
Cash paid for tax.
Remember, depreciation is a non-cash expense, so we ignore it in the direct method.

CFO by the indirect method:
1. Take the company's net income.
2. Remove any cash flow related to financing or investing activity because they are non-operating expenses. They will come under CFI and CFF.
3. Add any non-cash expense and minus any non-cash revenue.
4. Account for the sources and uses of cash as reflected in the changes to balance the accounts. When an asset increases,

it means we used cash, so subtract the change. When an asset decreases, the change is added. When a liability increases, we delay cash, so add the change. When a liability decreases, it means we used cash, so subtract the change.

5. Any losses incurred in the sale of assets, any losses experienced in the sale of investments, are added back because they are from investing activities. All the gains from these items must be subtracted.

6. Add all non-cash items like depreciation or amortization (of intangibles and bond discount).

Changes in the balance sheet

In this section, we will see how operating assets and liabilities change from period to period.

Operating assets are receivables, inventory, prepayments, deferred tax assets, etc. Operating liabilities are payables, both trade payables and internal payables, accrued expenses, and deferred tax liabilities.

Add back any decreases in operating assets or increases in operating liabilities because they are sources of cash. And subtract any increase in operating assets or decrease in operating liabilities because these are uses of cash.

Now, have a look at CFI and CFF

Investing activities:

We need to figure out how much money was spent during the period on new assets. For that, we need to look at the change in the asset account.

How much was the balance of the asset at the beginning of the period, and how much was there at the end?

Ending balance of the asset can be calculated as,
Beginning value of asset + money paid out for assets - money received in for assets sold = ending balance.

For each asset sold, we need to consider both the book value of the asset and the gain or loss on the sale. If the sale gave us gain, we need to add that amount to the book value. A loss would have to be removed from the book value to get to the cash proceeds on the sale.

CFF financing activities: This includes transactions related to the company's capital structure. We need to look at the company's interactions with its creditors and its shareholders. With the creditors, we may have inflows like the issuance of new debt. And outflows like repayment of existing debt. For the shareholders, we have inflows from equity issuance, and we have outflows for dividends and stock repurchases.

So, for creditors, the net effect on cash flow could be represented like this.

New borrowings - any principal repaid. We are only looking at principal repaid because we are assuming that we have covered interest payments as part of the CFO under IFRS.

For the shareholders, we have equity issued inflows minus outflows for share repurchases and dividends paid.

Converting cash flows from the indirect to the direct method.

CFI and CFF would be identical regardless of which method is chosen so we focus only on CFO.

Reason to convert from the indirect method to the direct method: The CFO constructed by the direct method is a more valuable resource for an analyst than one constructed by the indirect method.

There are three steps to this conversion.
1. Disaggregate net income into total revenues and total expenses. And take totals of net revenues and total expenses separately (the income statement and balance sheet will be given).

We simply take the income statement for incomes and take a total, and then separate out the expenses, and take a total. The net between those two figures should equal net income.
2. Disaggregated these two figures into their cash and non-cash components. Separate non-cash revenues from revenues and separate non-cash expenses from expenses.
3. Take the two cash components and build the CFO using the direct method from scratch. That means we're talking about cash collected from customers, cash paid to suppliers, employees, operating expenses, interest, and tax.

Analyzing reported and common-size cash flow statements

In this section, we are going to understand the company's cash flow situation.

Major sources and uses of cash: The uses and sources of cash of a firm are an important part of cash flow analysis. When a firm is at the start, it most probably generates negative cash flow from operations, and this might be financed by external sources of cash, such as investing and or financing activities. After some time, when the company is establishing itself, it must generate positive cash flows from operating activities so it can return the external financing.

Operating cash flow:
First of all, we look at the trends in working capital. Cash flow statements constructed by the indirect method show us how current assets (like inventory, receivables, payables, etc.) are changing over time, and this will give us a great idea of how operating cash flows are changing and why.

Interpretation: A positive operating cash flow is good if it is generated from operating activities. But positive cash flow is not good if it is being generated by selling current assets like inventory.

One important thing to note is that a cash flow figure higher (lower) than the net income indicates good (bad/ aggressive/ improper accounting) reporting quality.

Cash flow from investing activities: We need to consider each line item individually and find out what we have in uses of cash and sources of cash.

Uses of cash: Spending money on property, plant, and equipment, or maybe we are acquiring companies for cash, or investing in securities of other companies.

Sources of cash: Sources of cash in investing activities may be the sale of property, plant, and equipment, the sale of a business unit, etc.

Interpretation: The important thing to note with sales is why the company is selling assets. Are they selling to invest in a better opportunity, or are they generating cash to meet obligations?

Cash flow from financing activity:

This is also a study of the uses and sources of cash.

Uses of cash: The Company may be repurchasing its own stock or paying dividends to equity shareholders.

Sources of cash: Sources of cash in CFI might be the issuance of debt or equity. An analyst must examine why the company has a positive or negative cash flow here.

Interpretation: An outflow means a negative balance, which might be a good thing if the company is paying off debts, but an inflow (positive balance) might be a bad thing if the company needs to generate cash from financing activities to pay dividends. If this is the case, it means the company`s CFO are not sufficient.

Common-size analysis of the cash flow statement:

Just like the income statement and balance sheet, a common-size analysis of the cash flow statement can also be useful in understanding the company's cash flow.

We have 2 methods for developing the common-size cash flow statement.

1.   The inflow/outflow method (revenue-based method). 2. The percentage sales method (as we did with the income statement)

1.   The inflow/outflow method (revenue-based method): we take each inflow as a percentage of the total inflow and each outflow as a percentage of the total outflow.

This method shows where the concentration of cash inflow/outflow is. It is helpful to identify trends and future forecasting.

2.   The percentage sales method: We simply take each line item as a percentage of sales revenue from the income statement. It is helpful to identify trends and future forecasting.

Calculation and interpretation of free cash flow to the firm, free cash flow to equity, and performance and coverage cash flow ratios

Free cash flow (FCF): Free cash flow is the cash left after making capital expenditure (including growth). FCF is a measure of a company's financial performance, calculated as operating cash flow minus capital expenditures.
Two types of free cash flow. 1. Free cash flow to the firm and 2. Free cash flow to equity.

1. **Free cash flow to the firm:** It is the cash available for both equity and debt holders. It means the cash available for dividends and interest payments after deduction of operating expenses and capital investment. We calculate FCFC from operating cash flow as follows

FCFF = Cash Flow from Operations + Interest Expense x (1 - Tax Rate) – Capital expenditures. **Remember that we need to add back in the interest expense (and eliminate the tax rate effect).**

From net income, we can calculate free cash by using the following formula.

FCFF = net income + non-cash charges + interest x (1 - tax rate) - long-term investments - investments in working capital

We take net income, add back non-cash charges like depreciation and amortization, add back the after-tax interest expense, and then we remove capital expenditure and working capital investment. The result would be the same from both formulae.

Free cash flow to equity: **The** cash available just to the equity holders. It is the cash left after operating expenses, fixed capital investment, and borrowing costs. It shows how much cash is available to the equity shareholders of the company as dividends or stock buybacks, after all expenses, reinvestments, and debt repayments.

Calculation of FCFE: FCFE= CFO -net capital expenditure + net borrowings
Where Net borrowing = Debt issued – debt paid.
Cash flow ratios:
We are to discuss performance and coverage ratios.

Performance ratios:
Cash flow to revenue ratio: **Formula**; Cash flow to revenue ratio = CFO/ net revenues.
It tells us how much cash is generated per dollar of revenue.

Cash return on assets: **Formula:** CFO/ Average total assets. It tells us how much cash is generated per dollar of assets.

Cash return on equity: **Formula:** CFO/ Average shareholders' equity. It tells us how much cash is generated per dollar of shareholders' investment.

Cash flow to income ratio: **Formula:** CFO/ Operating income. It tells us the cash-generating ability from operations.

Cash flow per share: Formula; (CFO — preferred dividend)/Weighted average number of common shares.

Coverage ratios

Debt coverage ratio: Formula; CFO/ Total debt. It tells us about the company's financial risk and leverage.

Interest coverage ratio: Formula; (CFO + tax paid + interest paid)/ interest paid. It measures the company's ability to pay interest. Sometimes, under IFRS, interest paid is given under financing activity. Just take that interest and nothing else needs to be done.

Long-term Debt repayment ratio: Formula; CFO/ cash paid on long-term debt. It measures the company's ability to pay down debt obligations with operating cash flow.

Dividend payment ratio = CFO /dividends paid. It measures the company's ability to pay dividends out of operating cash.

Reinvestment ratio: formula; CFO/Long-term assets. It measures a firm's ability to acquire long-term assets by using the CFO.

The investing and financing ratio: Formula; CFO/ Cash outflow for investing and financing activities. It tells us about the firm's ability to satisfy debts, pay dividends, and make asset purchases.

Chapter 6: Financial analysis techniques

Tools and techniques used in financial analysis, their uses and limitations

There are several tools and techniques that are used to convert financial statements into formats that can be easily analyzed. <u>These are ratio analysis, common size analysis, graphical analysis, regression analysis, etc.</u>

These tools are very important when companies are not compatible because of different locations, or maybe they operate in different industries.

Ratio analysis benefits: Ratio analysis is used for
- Internal and external comparison.
- To project future earnings and cash flow.
- To evaluate a company's financial flexibility (ability to obtain cash) to meet its obligations and to grow even in difficult financial circumstances.
- To measure the performance of a company's management.
- To look at how the company or the industry is changing over time.
- To compare the company with its peer companies or relevant industry benchmarks.

Limitations of ratios: 1. They are not useful in isolation. They are only useful when they are combined with an overall <u>understanding of the company</u>, the company's industry, and the <u>macroeconomic environment.</u>

3. Ratio analysis is also not useful for big companies that have multiple sources of income from entirely different industries. Because of the complexity of the big company, relevant benchmarks won't be available.

4. Analysis based on a small subset of ratios might not be reliable because one set of financial ratios might indicate a certain level of performance, but another set of ratios on the same company might indicate that that performance level is not sustainable.
5. Ratios calculated from financial reports built on differing accounting standards may not be immediately comparable. (Accounting treatments differ in inventory evaluation, appreciation, and off-balance sheet items.)

Common size analysis: Common size is all about expressing financial data or entire financial statements relative to a single item.

Vertical common size balance sheets base everything relative to total assets. So total assets would be marked in the report as a hundred percent, and everything else is expressed as a percentage of that total assets figure. For example,

percentage of cash $= \frac{cash}{total\ asset} x100$

The benefits:
We can determine
- The company's financing sources. and
- How does the company's balance sheet differ from the industry norm?

Vertical common-size income statements are very similar to a vertical common-size balance sheet. In a vertical common-size income statement, everything is calculated as a percentage of total revenues. For example, Gross profit percentage = $\frac{Gross\ profit}{sales} x 100$.

Vertical common size reports, both the balance sheet and the income statement, are useful to an analyst performing a cross-sectional analysis. With cross-sectional analysis, we're comparing some metric of one company to that same metric from another company or to an industry benchmark.

For example, if one company has shown receivables on their vertical common size balance sheet at thirty-two percent of total assets, but another company or all of the companies in the industry are below ten percent.

We need to know what this company is doing differently. This requires more investigation.

<u>Horizontal common-size statements</u> state everything relative to a base year.

For example, if the total assets in the first year are a hundred twenty million dollars and in the next year they have total assets of a hundred and thirty million dollars.

The first year will be shown as a hundred percent, with the second year showing a hundred eight-point three percent. This format is useful for answering questions like how the relative position of the company is changing and how their management of receivables and payables was changing over time.

Horizontal common-size statements are useful for trend analysis.

XYZ corp. LTD
Income statement
For the year ended 31Dec.2xx9   **Vertical common-size income statement**

Sales	100	(1000/1000)x10000=	100%
COGS	600	600/1000)x100	60%
GP	400	(400/1000)x100(400/1000)x100=	40%
Operating exp	40	(40/1000)x100=	4%
Admin exp	30	(30/1000)x100=	3%
Tax Expense	10	(10/1000)x100=	1%
Net profit	320	(320/1000)x100=	32%

XYZ Corp. LTD
Balance sheet
As on 31Dec.2xx9

zontal common-size balance sheet taking 2xx6 as the base year

Year	2xx6	2xx7	2xx8	2xx6 (%)	2xx7 (%)	2xx8 %)
Assets						
Cash and cash equivalents	100	120	140	(100/100)x100= 100%	(120/100)x100 = 120%	140
Account receivables	80	90	100	(80/80) x100 =100	(90/80)x100 =112.5	125
Inventory	200	210	220	100	105	110
PP&E	1000	1000	1000	100	100	100
Total assets	**1380**	**1420**	**1460**	**100**	**102.89**	**105.79**
Liabilities						
Account payables	100	105	110	100	105	110
Interest payable	50	55	60	100	110	120
long term debt	700	730	760	100	104.2857143	108.5714

total liabilities	850	890	930		100	104.71	109.41
common equity	530	530	530		100	100	100
Total liabilities & Equity	1380	1420	1460		100	102.89%	105.79

Graphical analysis: Graphical analysis is building visual representations of financial information to aid in the understanding, comparison, or explanation of the company's financial performance. Some examples of graphical analysis tools are stacked bar graphs, pie charts, and line graphs. Each is useful in its own way for expressing information over different time periods and emphasizing different areas.

Regression analysis: Regression analysis is all about discovering a statistical relationship between two variables.

Common example is sales to GDP. Can we draw a significantly consistent relationship between how the company's sales change in relation to real GDP?

Classification, calculation, and interpretation of activity, liquidity, solvency, profitability, and valuation ratios

We have five classifications of ratios.
1. Activity ratios: 2. Liquidity ratios   3. Solvency ratios
   4. Profitability ratios 5. Valuation ratios.
Note: These classifications are not mutually exclusive.

Activity ratios
Activity ratios are also called asset utilization ratios or operating efficiency ratios. These ratios measure a firm's ability

to manage its assets. We have the following ratios in this category.

Receivable turnover ratio: How efficiently a firm controls receivables is measured by **receivable turnover ratio**.
Receivable turnover ratio = Annual sales/ average receivables.
This ratio should be closer to industry norms.
One thing must be remembered here is that whenever we use balance sheet data with income statement or cash flow data in a ratio, the balance sheet figure must be taken as an average by adding the opening and ending balances and dividing by 2.

Number of days sales are outstanding or average collection period: It is the average number of days taken by the customers to pay the firm.
No. of days sales outstanding = 365/ receivable turnover
This ratio should be close to industry norms. If it is too high it means the firm is not collecting cash easily (inefficiency). A ratio too low shows a very strict credit policy, which might be affecting sales, or the firm is collecting cash very efficiently.

Inventory turnover ratio = Cost of goods sold/ average inventory
It measures a firm's efficiency in inventory management and its processing. It tells how many times the firm has sold its inventory completely (theoretically).

Days inventory in hand = 365/ inventory turnover
It tells us how many days a firm takes to process its inventory. Again, these (Inventory turnover and Days inventory in hand) should be close to industry norms. A higher inventory turnover ratio means fewer days of inventory on hand. It might

indicate a highly effective inventory management, or the company is not holding enough stock and is potentially on the verge of shortages and falling sales revenue. Analysts must see revenue growth to assess the explanation. A higher (or same as industry) growth with high turnover means effective inventory management, and vice versa. A lower inventory turnover means a higher number of days inventory in hand, which may indicate that there is too much capital tied up and a high processing time. It means the inventory could be getting obsolete. The cost of goods sold may not be according to current circumstances.

Payable turnover ratio = purchases/ average payables: It means how many times the company pays its payables completely (theoretically).

Number of days of payables = 365/ payable turnover ratio

These two should be close to industry norms. A relatively higher payables turnover (which would mean a relatively lower number of days payables are outstanding), the company might not be effectively taking advantage of credit facilities made available to them, or they might be taking advantage of early payment discounts. We must look at the liquidity ratios to get a proper understanding. If a company has better liquidity ratios but higher days payable (lower payable turnover), it means they are taking advantage of available credit facilities. If the liquidity position is bad with lower payable turnover, they might be having trouble with cash generation.

Working capital turnover = Total sales/ average working capital. Working capital is the difference between current assets and current liabilities.

It tells us how efficiently the company is turning its working capital investment into sales revenue. It indicates how much revenue the company is generating per dollar of working capital investment. For example, if working capital turnover is 5, it means for every dollar of working capital we generate, five dollars of sales revenue. A zero or negative value of this ratio is not usable.

The fixed asset turnover = Sales revenue by/ Average net fixed assets

It tells us how efficiently investment in fixed assets is being turned into sales revenue.

Interpretation: A Higher figure would indicate efficient use of fixed assets. A lower number may indicate inefficiency in business because it requires a large capital investment. Or it is a newborn company that has not yet reached its full capacity.

Total asset turnover = Sales revenue / average total assets

It tells us how efficiently the company is generating revenue from its assets.

Interpretation: A higher figure indicates that the company is effectively or efficiently utilizing its assets to generate revenue. A lower figure would indicate inefficiencies or that the firm is in a very capital-intensive business.

Liquidity ratios

Liquidity ratios measure a company's ability to meet its short-term obligations.

We have 3 major liquidity ratios, the current ratio, the quick ratio, and the cash ratio.

Current ratio = Current assets /current liabilities.

Quick ratio = Liquid assets / current liabilities. Where, Liquid assets = cash+ marketable sec. + receivables

Cash ratio = (cash + marketable securities) / current liabilities.

Interpretations

A current ratio of one indicates that the company's current assets are equal to the dollar value of its current liabilities. So, the short-term obligations are just covered. A ratio less than one means that the company is relying on operating profit to meet short-term obligations because current assets are not enough.

The same interpretation is for the following ratios, too.

The quick ratio is a more realistic approach to a company's ability to convert certain current assets into cash. Pre-payments, for example, might be included in the current assets of a company but would be very difficult to turn into cash. The same is the case with inventory. So, we exclude these two from the quick ratio to have more meaningful results.

With the cash ratio, we are more conservative about the asset's ability to meet short-term obligations. We only include most liquid assets. We only include cash and marketable securities that the company has right now to pay its short-term obligations.

Other liquidity ratios: The defensive interval and the cash conversion cycle.

Defensive interval = (cash + marketable securities + receivables)/ average daily expenditures

It is a measure of how long the company can continue paying its liabilities with current assets, assuming no new inflows.

For example, a defensive interval of 40 means the company can survive the current pace for 40 days without getting any cash inflow. A higher number indicates greater liquidity.

Cash conversion cycle = {(days sales outstanding) +days inventory in hand) – (Number of days of payables)}

It is the time it takes for a company to turn a product into cash (from inventory to receivable to cash collection).

A shorter time means greater liquidity. It should be compared with industry norms.

Solvency ratios:

Solvency ratios measure a company's ability to meet longer-term obligations. This category is most relevant to analysts interested in a company's financial leverage and its ability to service long-term debt.

Solvency ratios typically have two categories.

1. Debt ratios   2. Coverage ratios

Debt ratios

Debt to equity =Total debt / total equity.

This ratio compares the debt side of the capital structure to the equity side. It shows how much debt a company is using to finance its assets in comparison to equity. A higher figure would indicate a less solvent company.

Debt to assets ratio = total debt / total assets.

This ratio compares the company's debt position to the value of its total assets. It tells us the percentage of total assets financed by debt (all liabilities). A higher ratio indicates weak solvency.

Debt to capital ratio = Total debt / (total debt + shareholders' equity).

Total debt means all interest-bearing short and long-term debt. Equity includes common stock and preferred stock. It shows how much capital is financed by debt. A higher ratio indicates weak solvency.

Financial leverage = Average total assets / average total equity.

A higher ratio here indicates the company is using a higher proportion of debt to finance its assets, which indicates risk.

Coverage ratios

There are two major coverage ratios, the interest coverage ratio and the fixed charge coverage ratio.

Interest coverage ratio = EBIT/interest payment

EBIT is earnings before interest and taxes. It measures how many times a company's earnings before interest and tax cover its interest obligations.

A higher number is desirable here because it indicates that the earnings are quite larger than the interest payment. A lower ratio means they have difficulty in paying interest.

Fixed charge coverage = (EBIT + lease payments) / (interest expense plus lease payments).

It tells us how well the company's fixed outflows are covered by its earnings. A higher ratio indicates the company is in a better position and vice versa.

Profitability ratios

Profitability ratios measure the overall performance of the firm in terms of revenues, assets, capital, and equity.

Before the profitability ratios, we need a good understanding of the structure of the income statement.

Net sales revenue - cost of goods sold = gross profit.

Gross profit -operating expenses = operating profit EBIT = earnings before interest and taxes

EBIT- interest = earnings before tax= EBT

EBT- taxes = earnings after tax.

Earnings after tax – other items = net income before dividends.

Total capital = long-term debt + short-term debt + common equity + preferred equity.

Some analysts may use total assets for total capital if they want to include things like accounts payable.

Now let's look at the profitability ratio.
We have two categories of profitability ratios

1. Ratios based on the company's sales revenue 2.   Ratios based on capital invested.

Ratios based on the company's sales revenue

Gross profit margin = gross profit/revenues.

Gross profit margin indicates the amount of profit left over after accounting for the cost of goods sold. It is a comparison of Gross profit with sales. A higher gross profit margin indicates a company's ability to charge a higher price for a product that they can manufacture for a lower cost and vice versa. Gross profit margin also helps the management in cost control.

Operating profit margin = Operating profit/sales revenues.

We know that operating profit is gross profit minus operating costs. While analyzing operating profit margin, it's customary to compare the trend of operating Margin with gross margin.

If the operating profit margin is improving faster than the gross profit margin, then the company may be getting more efficient in bringing down the operating cost.

Pretax margin = earnings before tax/sales revenue.

This is another measure of profitability. An analyst should be careful to consider whether the item driving a change in pretax margin is likely to continue into the future or if it's a one-time event (due to non-recurring items).

Ratios based on capital invested
Return on assets =Net income / average total assets.

It tells us how much income the company has earned per dollar of assets. This is a better measure of how they performed by taking their size into consideration. The main problem with this ratio is that net income is a return for only equity holders (both common and preferred), but for most companies, assets are financed by both equity and debt.

To eliminate this drawback and account for debt holders' profitability, an analyst might use operating return on assets, calculated as

ROA = (Net income + interest expense (1-tax rate)} / average total assets.

Return on total capital = EBIT/Average total capital

Total capital is short-term and long-term debt, and common and preferred equity. In this ratio, we measure the return on each dollar of capital invested. A very low ratio from industry norms should alarm the analyst.

Return on equity (or return on total equity) = Net income / average total equity.

This ratio focuses on the equity holders, including preferred equity. It should also be according to industry norms. A very low ratio must concern analysts.

Return on common equity = Net income – preferred dividends)/average common equity

While

Net income – preferred dividends = income available to common stockholders.

This ratio measures the return just to the common shareholders and compares that figure to the capital invested by just the common shareholders.

Valuation ratios

Valuation ratios are all about ownership and the benefit of ownership. These ratios are ratios like price to earnings, price to cash flow, price to sales, and price to book value.

This stuff is all covered later on in the equity material, and even some of it later on in this section.

Relationships among ratios and company evaluation

Let's have an example to relate ratios and company evaluation.

Sample balance sheet

Year	Current	vious
Assets	000$	000$
Cash and equivalents	50	40
Trade receivables	70	60
inventory	210	200
total current assets	**330**	**300**
Property plant and equipment	2000	2000
Accumulated depreciation	300	295
Net property plant and equipment	1700	1720
Total assets	**2030**	**2020**
Liabilities		
Trade payables	114	113
Current portion of long-term debt	70	65
Short-term debt	130	125
Total current liabilities	**314**	**295**
Long-term debt	590	610
Deferred tax	116	110
Common stock at par	260	260
Additional paid-up capital	500	500
Retained earnings	250	245
Total shareholders' equity	1010	1005
Total liabilities and equity	**2030**	**2020**

Sample income statement

Year	Current	previous
Sales	10000	**9500**
Cost of goods sold	9000	8600
Gross profit	1000	900
Operating expenses	560	540
EBIT	440	360
Interest expense	40	35
EBT	400	325
Taxes	55	52
Net income	345	273
Common dividend	245	173

Ratios	Current	Previous	industry benchmark
Current ratio	1.05	1.016949153	1.1
Quick ratio	0.38	0.338983051	1
cash ratio	0.1592357	0.169491525	0.7
inventory turnover	43.902439	41.95121951	42
days inventory in hand	8.3138889	8.700581395	8
receivable turnover	153.84615	146.1538462	150
days sales outstanding	2.3725	2.497368421	1.5

Now let's look at what these ratios are telling us about this company.

Firstly, in terms of the <u>current ratio,</u>

The current ratio is increasing which suggests that current assets are increasing relative to current liabilities. Meaning that the company is improving its liquidity position. Moreover, it is also close to the industry benchmark.

But the quick ratio doesn't look so good. Although it has increased slightly, it is still very low compared to the industry benchmark. It tells us that we do not have sufficient liquid assets.

If we have only two ratios, it is fair to comment that the company`s liquidity is not good, and the inventory is misleading the current ratio.

Now, if we bring in the days' sales outstanding figures we just calculated, we can see a decline from 2.4 days to 2.3 days. This suggests that the company is collecting cash on its receivables a bit quicker than they were before, which is a positive sign, but it is still greater than the industry.

Days inventory in hand is also improving and is very close to industry norms.

Putting all of that together, it looks like although this company's inventory and receivable ratios are good, their liquidity position is actually weakening.

Calculation, Application, and interpretation of DU Pont analysis of return on equity

DuPont analysis: It is a method used to analyze a company's return on equity. In this, we can use algebra to break the simple return on equity formula and find out what is driving return on equity.

The basic formula: *return on equity= Net income / average equity.*

If we multiply above and below the line by sales revenue and rearrange it, we come up with the following formula.

$$ROE= \left\{\frac{Net\ income}{Sale}\right\} \times \left(\frac{sales}{Average\ equity}\right)$$

And again, by total assets, we end up with a formula that looks like this.

$$ROE= \left\{\frac{Netincome}{sale}\right\} \times \left\{\frac{Sales}{Total\ assets}\right\} \times \left\{\frac{Total\ assets}{Average\ equity}\right\}$$

The first part, net income over sales, is the company's net profit margin; the second part, sales over assets, is the company's asset turnover, and the third part, assets over equity, is the company's leverage ratio, also known as the equity multiplier.

One important thing to realize here is that if we combine these first two parts, we end up with net income over assets, which is return on assets. Now, in terms of interpretation, we have looked at these metrics to some extent already.

Net profit margin measures the company's ability to generate profits from its ordinary business activity. A higher number here indicates the company is in a good position in their industry.

Asset turnover gives us a measure of how the company is able to generate sales from its assets. This is a valuable comparison mechanism that can be used to compare companies of different sizes. Again, a higher figure indicates a better-performing company.

With financial leverage, we're looking at the company's financial risk and solvency.

Comparing the company's assets to its equity position is just the same as comparing liabilities plus equity to the equity position. It is a measure of what proportion of the capital structure this company holds on the liability side. A higher number here indicates a company with more obligations, more risk, and a greater chance of insolvency.

DuPont analysis can be extended by further breaking down the first term, the net profit margin. For this part, we multiply by EBT/EBT and EBIT/EBIT and rearrange to end up with a form that looks like this.

ROE= {Net income/ EBT} x {EBT/ EBIT} x {EBIT/ Sales} x {sales/Average assets} x {Average assets/ average equity}

Now we already know these last two components are asset turnover and the leverage ratio, so those are interpreted the same as we had before.

This first term, Net income over earnings before tax is known as the tax burden. Earnings before tax over EBIT is also known as the company's interest burden, which gives us an indication of how the company's interest expense changes relative to earnings.

The term EBIT over sales is called the EBIT margin. This figure tells us how much the company`s revenues come from their operating profit, so how much is based on their everyday business activity.

Ratios used in equity analysis and credit analysis.

Equity analysis: In equity analysis, we evaluate and compare the performance of a company from the perspective of an investor.
The major question is whether I would include this company in a portfolio.

First of all, we need to be aware of some useful per-share quantities.

Basic earnings per share: The Income the company has generated for each common share outstanding.
Basic EPS= {Net income - the distributions to preferred shareholders}/ weighted average number of common shares outstanding.
Be careful, EPS in isolation is not the most valuable comparison metric. It heavily depends on the number of outstanding shares.

Diluted EPS: It is the EPS if all convertible instruments were converted into common stock. There will be an income adjustment needed, and the number of common shares will have to change to reflect the conversion.

Cash flow per share = CFO / weighted average number of common shares.

Book value per share =Book value of ordinary equity / weighted average number of common shares.
It tells us what a common shareholder might get in the event of liquidation.

Now we can use these per-share values to calculate valuation ratios.

We are going to look at price to earnings, price to cash flow, and price to book. Each is calculated by taking the price per share and dividing it by the relevant per share value we calculated before.

Price-to-earnings reflects the cost to an investor of partaking in the earnings generated by the company.

Price to cash flow assesses the amount that an investor has to pay for each dollar of cash flow generated by the company, and this metric is useful as an alternative to price earnings and is especially useful in cases where reported earnings are of questionable quality.

Price-to-book value is the cost paid by an investor per dollar of the company's book value. It's often interpreted as a comparison between the company's expected future return and the return required by the market. If this ratio is greater than one, we would expect the company to generate a rate of return in excess of the market's required return.

Dividend-related ratios

The dividend payout ratio = amount of dividend declared/ net income available to common shareholders.

It is a measure of the amount of earnings that are distributed to shareholders.

Retention rate = {net income available to common shareholders -dividend declared}/ net income available to common shareholders

It is a measure of the amount of the company's earnings that were not distributed to shareholders.

Sustainable growth rate = (Retention rate) x (return on equity).

It measures the company's ability to finance its own growth through its ordinary business activities.

Specific ratios

These ratios give us a general idea, but there are other specific ratios related to a specific industry. Financial services companies, for example, are supposed to follow some specific regulations. For these types of companies, ratios like capital adequacy under the monetary reserve requirement are important.

In the service industry, we might be interested in net income per employee or sales per employee ratios.

In the retail industry, sales per square foot are important.

Coefficient of variation metrics

We can measure riskiness of different financial statements items like coefficient of variation of sales (CV sales = $\frac{\text{Standard deviation of sales}}{\text{mean } sales}$) and CV of net income (CV of net income $= \frac{\text{SD net income}}{\text{mean } net\ income}$) etc.

Credit analysis

Credit analysis is an assessment of the ability of a company to repay its debts. In this, we measure the credit risk of a company, its creditworthiness, and its credit risk.

In credit assessment, we base our analysis on the interest coverage ratio, the debt to asset ratio, the return on capital ratio, the cash flow to debt ratio, etc. These ratios tell us about the company's ability to repay debts from core business activities.

Segment reporting and segment ratios

Business segment is a portion of a larger company that accounts for more than ten percent of overall assets or revenues and is distinguishable from the rest of the business.

A company must disclose separate information about any operating entity that meets these criteria.

Although companies are not required to publish financial statements for each of their business segments, some amount of segmented reporting is a requirement of both IFRS and U. S. GAAP.

Some of the disclosures that are required for each reportable segment include

- A statement of profit or loss.
- A measure of the assets and liabilities of the segment.
- A report distinguishing between revenue from external customers and revenue from other segments.
- Asset costs and depreciation or amortization expenses.
- Other information related to interest payments, interest revenue, and tax, based on the information disclosed.

And analysts can generate some useful ratios like

- Segment margins.
- Assets turned over.
- The segments return on assets.

And with those, we can assess the performance of the segment individually to get some more detail on the overall company's performance.

Ratio analysis and other techniques to model and forecast earnings.

If sales revenue forecasts are given, analysts can use historical data and trend analysis to forecast certain elements of financial statements, like gross profit.

Forecasts are generally a distribution of possible outcomes (and not a single point estimate). In forecast building, techniques like sensitivity analysis (analysis of changes in inputs), Scenario analysis, and Assimilation are used.

Sensitivity analysis: Sensitivity analysis is based on what-if conditions. For example, what would happen to gross profit if the cost of goods sold changes by 1 percent?

Scenario analysis: Analyzing the effect of a change in a set of input variables.

Assimilation: Taking a distribution of inputs to yield a distribution of outputs.

Chapter 7: Inventories

Costs associated with inventories and costs recognized as expenses

In inventory accumulation, certain costs are required to be capitalized, and others are to be expensed.

The capitalized costs are added to the inventory value in the balance sheet. These costs are expensed when the inventory is sold.

The expensed costs go into the income statement for that period. Note that these would not be part of COGS. These are expenses incurred in the accumulation of inventory that is not being capitalized.

Costs that would be capitalized are called product costs. Product cost = purchase price - discount or rebate + relevant labor costs + overheads + any other costs incurred in bringing the inventory to its current location in its current condition.

The costs to be expensed are called period costs. This would include any abnormal waste in materials, labor or overheads. Any storage costs that are not required in the production chain, any costs of administration, and any costs involved in making sales.

Different inventory valuation methods

In this section, we are to look for inventory valuation. How do we value the inventory that we have available for sale?

Under IFRS, the methodology chosen for valuing inventory is called the cost flow formula. While under U. S. GAAP, it is known as the cost flow assumption.
Under IFRS, we have three methods for valuing inventory.
- Specific identification
- weighted average
- First in first out.

US GAAP, we also have these three methods permitted under IFRS, but we are also allowed to use last-in, first-out.

Specific identification method: Under this method, each item in the firm's inventory is matched with its own original cost. When an item is sold, accounting for its cost is based on the actual cost of bringing that individual item into the company's inventory. A company that works with a relatively smaller inventory with costly items or very individual or unique items, it is the most appropriate method.
Jewelers, for example, would use specific identification to account for the cost of their stock.

Weighted average cost method: The weighted average cost method is a very simple idea. We take the total cost of inventory and divide by the number of units available for sale. That gives us the average per unit cost.
We can use that per unit cost to calculate the inventory value by multiplying by the number of units available for sale,

or we can calculate the cost of goods sold by multiplying by the number of units sold.

First in, first out method: The FIFO method. With this method, we assume that the oldest item in inventory is sold first. We sell items in the order that they were brought into stock. But this has two major effects on the financial statements.

1. Because the oldest items are the ones being sold, the cost of goods sold will be based on some potentially much older stock. This means potentially much older pricing.
2. Because the items remaining in inventory are newer stock, which were purchased more recently, their value may be closer to the current market value, so in essence, what we're going to get is a cost of goods sold figure, which might be out of date.

Last in, first out LIFO method: This is the opposite of the FIFO method. When the inventory is sold, it is the most recently purchased items that are sold first. The effect of this is that now the cost of goods sold figure will more accurately reflect current market prices, while inventory valuation will be based on some potentially older prices. So, we have a more accurate cost of goods sold and a potentially out-of-date inventory evaluation.

Cost of sales, Gross profit, and ending inventory using different inventory valuation methods and using perpetual and periodic inventory systems

Let's say, for example, a company has 200 units in stock at the beginning of the period with a per-unit cost of 2$. During the period, they have one order for 100 units at 2.5$ and a second order of 150 more units at per unit cost 3$.

We're going to calculate the cost of goods sold and inventory value at the period end using the three methods.

Assuming that a total of 400 units were sold during the period, leaving 50 units remaining.

Weighted average method: With the weighted average method, the first task is to calculate the weighted average cost per unit.

$$Weighted\ average\ cost\ of\ inventory$$

$$= \frac{\sum_{1}^{n} X_iP_i}{total\ units\ purchased} = \frac{400+250+450}{200+100+150} = 2.44\$$$

Where x is the number of units purchased and p is the price. We multiply the number of units purchased by their price and sum up. Then we divide this sum by the total units purchased, and the result would be our weighted average cost of each unit purchased.

Opening inventory	200 units @2 $	400 $
Purchased	100 @ 2.5$	250$
Purchased	150 @ 3$	450$
Cost of goods available for sale	(200 +100 + 150) * 2.44 = 1098	
Ending inventory	50 * 2.44 = 122	
Cost of goods sold	**1098 – 122 = 976**	

Let's say we have total sales revenues of $1500, then our gross profit will be $1500 – 976= 524$.

FIFO: With the first-in-first-out method, we sold the units from the oldest boxes in stock first, even when we had newer boxes available.

That means first we sold 200 units that were purchased at s$/ unit. Then we sold 100 units that were purchased at 2.5$/unit. Lastly, we sold 100 units of 3$/unit. So we are left with 50 units bought at 3$. So the calculation is as follows.

Opening inventory	200 units @2 $	400 $	Sold 200 units of 2$
Purchased	100 @ 2.5$	250$	Sold 100 units of 2.5$
Purchased	150 @ 3$	450$	Sold 100 units of 3$
Cost of goods available for sale	(400 +250 + 450) = 1100		
Ending inventory	50 *3 = 150$		
Cost of goods sold	1100 – 150 = 950		

Let's say we have total sales revenues of $1500, then our gross profit will be $1500 – 950= 550$.

LIFO: Last in, first out: The last in, first out method is only allowed under U. S. GAAP. It is not permitted under IFRS.

Opening inventory	200 units @2 $	400 $
Purchased	100 @ 2.5$	250$
Purchased	150 @ 3$	450$
Cost of goods available for sale	(400 +250 + 450) = 1100	
Ending inventory	50 *2 = 100$	
Cost of goods sold	1100 – 100 = 1000$	

Let's say we have total sales revenues of $1500, then our gross profit will be $1500 – 1000= 500$.

When we compare these three methods in terms of their effect on gross profit, we need to look at the cost of goods sold figure side by side while considering the pattern of the purchase price.

We are not given specific information on the dates of the orders here, so we can't really paint an accurate picture of the price trend, but we can at least say that the prices are increasing.

With rising prices, FIFO produces the lowest cost of goods sold figure.

The weighted average is the average, while LIFO produces the highest.

Now, given that gross profit is given by taking the cost of goods sold away from net sales revenue. This will mean that again under rising prices.

FIFO will produce the highest gross profit, LIFO the lowest, with weighted average somewhere in between.

Perpetual and periodic systems are the two most common ways that a company will record changes in inventory.

Perpetual system: In this method, inventory and cost of goods sold are continuously updated.

Sale and purchase transactions are recorded directly in inventory and cost of goods sold, so there's no need for a purchases account.

Periodic inventory system: The values of inventory and cost of goods sold are determined at the end of an accounting period. No detailed account is maintained. The inventory purchased during a year is reported in the purchases account. At the end of each period, purchases are added to the opening inventory to determine the cost of goods sold.

Let's take a look at an example of how this works. Here we have some purchases and sales data for a company's first quarter of business.

Purchases	5000	3.5$per unit
sales	2100	7 $ /unit
sales	1700	7 $ /unit
purchases	5000	4.5$ /unit
sales	1500	7$ /unit
sales	1800	7$ /unit

We're going to assume that they had no inventory on hand at the beginning of the period. We are going to analyze the effect of choosing between the perpetual and periodic inventory systems.

To perform this analysis, step one is to calculate sales revenue. This is going to be the same under both methods. Step two, then, is to calculate ending inventory. Step three is to use ending inventory to calculate cost of goods sold. And finally, the next step is to use sales revenue and cost of goods sold to get gross profit.

1. Sales revenue. Add all the sold units. It will be 7100 units. Each of these units was sold for seven dollars, so the company's total sales revenue =7100 x 7 =49700$.

Next, let's go through steps two, three, and four using the perpetual system and the LIFO method.

2. To calculate the value of closing inventory, we need to figure out the makeup of inventories as it exists at the end of the period.

units	Per unit	Available units
5000	3.5$	5000@3.5
-2100		(5000-2100 =) 2900 @3.5

-1700		(2900- 1700)= 1200@3.5
5000	4.5$	1200 @ 3.5 and 5000 @4.5
-1500		1200 @3.5 and 3500@4.5
-1800		1200 @3.5 and 1700 @4.5

Working through the purchase and sale transactions, we find that this company ends up with 1200 units at the 3.5 price level and 1700 units at the 4.5 price level.

So, the total value of ending inventory is = (1200x3.5) + (1700x4.5) =11850$

The next step is to calculate the cost of goods sold. To do that, we first need to calculate the total cost of purchased goods.

This is simply a case of pulling out the purchase transactions, multiplying the number of units by the price per unit, and taking a total.

Here we have a total cost of purchase = (5000x3.5) + (5000x4.5) =40000$

So, cost of goods sold = cost of purchase – value of ending inventory = 40000 – 11850= 28150$

The last step then is to calculate gross profit for the perpetual system.

Gross profit = Sales revenues- cost of goods sold= 49700-28150= 21550$

Periodic method with LIFO: Since we know that sales revenue is the same as before, we can go straight to step 2, the value of ending inventory. This system is a bit different. All we need to do here is go through the purchase and sale transactions to find out how many units are remaining at the end of the period. We then apply the cost price of the oldest purchase transaction as the value for all remaining units.

Now our ending units are 5000 -2100 -1700 +5000 -1500 - 1800 = 2900, which costs 3.5@ (the oldest are remained with the oldest cost.) So, the cost of ending inventory is 2900 x 3.5 =10150.

Now, if we had more than 5000 units in closing inventory, then we wouldn't be able to use that price of 3.5 on its own because only 5000 units were ever available at that price.

{For example, if we had 6000 units remaining, we would take 5000 units at the price of 3.5$, the oldest price, and the other 1000 units would be taken out at a cost level from the next oldest price level of 4.5$ in line with the last in first principle.}

Following on that we need to calculate the cost of goods sold. With the periodic system, we work our way through the sales data using the most recent cost price of 4.5$ until we have accounted for 500 units.

After that, we move on to the older 3.5$ price.

In this case, we have 5000 units, which will be accounted for using the newer 4.5 price, and 2100 units, which will be accounted for using the older 3.5 price.

So, COGS= (5000x 4.5) x 2100x3.5= 29850$.
And, Gross profit = Sales-COGS= 49700-29850=19850

How do these figures compare side by side using the two methods?

	Perpetual	Periodic
Sales	49700	49700
Ending inventory	11850	10150
COGS	28150	29850

| Gross profit | 21550 | 19850 |

How inflation and deflation of inventory costs affect the financial statements and ratios of companies that use different inventory valuation methods

When prices are rising (inflation), LIFO will give us a higher cost of goods sold and a lower value of inventory on hand. It's because the most recent units are sold first, which are costly than older units. It means less gross profit and net profit will be reported in the income statement.

With increasing prices, FIFO will give us a lower cost of goods sold but a higher inventory on hand. This is because the older units with cheaper prices are sold first, while the newer units (with higher prices) will be kept in stock. It means we would be having higher gross and net profits than the LIFO method.

When prices are falling (deflation), the pattern will be the other way around. In this situation, LIFO gives us less cost of goods sold and higher inventory on hand, resulting in higher gross and net profits.

FIFO will give us higher COGS, lower inventory on hand, and lower gross and net profits.

Also, with rising prices, LIFO gives us a lower tax expense as COGS would be higher.

LIFO reserve and LIFO liquidation
Converting financial statements from LIFO to FIFO

We know that the ending inventory value is lower under LIFO than under FIFO. When a company reports under LIFO, they are required to report the LIFO reserve.

LIFO reserve is the amount by which LIFO inventory is lower than FIFO inventory. This reserve is maintained to allow ease of comparison among companies using LIFO and FIFO.

To compare financial statements prepared under LIFO with those prepared under FIFO, an analyst must

- Add LIFO reserve to LIFO inventory on the balance sheet
- Add LIFO reserve in retained earnings

There is another problem here. When LIFO is used in rising prices, the company has lower earnings, so it pays lower tax. SO, the company has more cash and retained earnings must also be adjusted accordingly. So, the analyst must minus LIFO reserve x tax rate from cash (on the balance sheet). And retained earnings are also increased by the LIFO reserve (1-tax rate) instead of the full LIFO reserve.

For comparison analyst must also convert LIFO COGS into FIFO COGS. The difference between LIFO COGS and FIFO COGS is the change in the LIFO reserve account. So, FIFO COGS LIFO COGS − {LIFO reserve at end of period -LIFO reserve at beginning of period}.

In case of falling prices, the difference between the LIFO ending and beginning amount would be negative. In this case, this will be added into LIFO COGS to convert it into FIFO COGS.

Challenge Question: ABC Limited is using the LIFO method of inventory. They reported ending inventory of $5 m in 2xx7 and of $4 m $ in 2xx8. COGS for the year 2xx8 are 10m$. LIFO reserve was 0.5 m in 2xx7 and 0.8m in 2xx8. Convert the inventory and COGS of 2xx8 from LIFO to FIFO.

Effects on Ratios

We assume an increase in prices while looking at the effects of adjustments from LIFO to FIFO on ratios.

Profitability ratios: LIFO produces higher COGS than FIFO and lower earnings. So, conversion from LIFO to FIFO gives us higher profitability ratios. For example, higher gross, operating, and net profit margins as compared to LIFO.

Liquidity: In comparison to FIFO, LIFO gives us a lower inventory value on the balance sheet because inventory is higher under FIFO. **The current ratio** is also higher under FIFO (because current assets are higher). Working capital is also higher under FIFO (working capital = current assets – current liabilities, and current assets are higher).

The quick ratio is unaffected by the firm's chosen inventory method because inventory is excluded from its numerator.

Activity ratios: We know that COGS are higher and inventory is lower under LIFO, so Inventory turnover (COGS / average inventory) is also higher than FIFO. So, when we convert it from LIFO to FIFO, we get a lower inventory turnover ratio. When we get lower inventory turnover, it means higher days of inventory in hand, as (365 / inventory turnover).

Solvency ratios: LIFO gives us lower total assets (because inventory is lower) than FIFO, so when we convert from LIFO to FIFO, we get higher total assets and higher stockholders' equity (assets – liabilities).

Because total assets and stockholders' equity are higher under FIFO, the debt-to-equity ratio is lower under FIFO.

Measurement of inventory at the lower of cost or net realizable value.

In this section, we are to look at the measurement of inventory value under IFRS and U. S. GAAP

Under IFRS, *we must value inventory at the lower of cost or net realizable value.*

Net realizable value = expected sales price - completion costs - selling costs.

If the cost is lower than the net realizable value, then it must be recorded at cost. And if subsequently, net realizable value falls below cost, the value of inventory must then be written down to account for that loss in value. And that loss would have to be reflected on the income statement.

After being written down, if the realizable value subsequently increases again. IFRS allows us to reverse the original right down that took us from the original cost level down to the lower net realizable value level. So, we post an increase to the inventory account and the gain to the income statement. It is known as a reversal of a right down.

These transactions would generally occur in a contra account called a valuation allowance account so that changes in value are kept separate from initial cost.

Under US GAAP, inventory is valued at the lower of cost or market.

Market value = replacement cost (but cannot be greater than Net realizable value). Or

Market value < NRV - normal profit margin.

If replacement cost >NRV, then the market is the net realizable value. If the replacement cost is NRV - normal profit margin, then the market is NRV -normal profit margin.

Again, in this case where the current market value was below the reported valuation of inventory, a write-down is performed and a loss is recognized on the income statement.

But U. S. GAAP does not allow write-ups or reversals in the case of a subsequent increase in value.

One interesting point to note is that because firms reporting inventory levels based on the LIFO method will have their inventory value based on older and likely lower cost levels. They will be less likely to experience a right down.

Valuing inventory at net realizable value for financial statements and ratios

When we write down inventory to net realizable value, it affects financial statements in many ways, as follows
- Inventory is included in current assets; a decrease in inventory will decrease current assets and also total assets.
- A decrease in total assets causes an increase in total asset turnover **(Sales / Average Total Assets) and debt to assets ratio.**
- Inventory turnover (COGS/ Average inventory) increases, but days inventory in hand and cash conversion cycle decrease.
- Shareholders' equity decreased, so the debt-to-equity ratio increases.
- Due to an increase in COGS, gross profit margin, operating profit margin, and net profit margin decrease.

- Percentage decrease in net income is often more than the percentage decrease in assets and or equity. So, return on assets and return on equity decrease.
- The current ratio (current assets/ current liabilities) decreases. No effect on the quick ratio, as we do not include inventory in it.
- In subsequent years, the written down COGS may decrease as we have lower inventory value, so the profit margins will increase, and so the ROA and ROE.

Financial statement presentation and disclosures relating to inventories

Disclosures related to inventory

Under IFRS and US GAAP, companies are required to disclose the following
- Accounting policies followed related to measurement. (It means the valuation method and cost flow formula).
- Carrying value by classification. (That means a breakdown of inventory value split out into raw materials, production supplies, works in progress, and finished units ready for sale).
- The value of units held at fair value less selling costs.
- The cost of goods sold or cost of sales.
- Any write-downs recognized in the period.
- Any reversals of write-downs recognized in the period.
- The circumstances leading to write-downs or reversals (GAAP does not allow reversals).
- Any inventory pledged as collateral against liabilities.

Changes in inventory

A firm can change inventory cost flow methods normally retrospectively (the previous year's financial statements are restated using the new cost flow method). There is an exception to this rule when a firm changes its inventory method to LIFO. In this case, the change is applied prospectively. It means changes in previous periods are not required for re-adjustments.

Under IFRS, the firm must explain that the change will provide reliable and more relevant information. Under U.S. GAAP, the firm must explain why the change in inventory method is preferable.

Issues to consider while examining a company's inventory disclosures and other sources of information

Some firms, like wholesalers and retailers (also called merchandising firms), do not manufacture goods. They only buy and sell. Their goods are ready for sale. So, they record inventory in one account only in the balance sheet.

Other firms that manufacture goods record goods in usually three accounts: raw material, work in process, and finished goods.

An analyst must use this information about inventory along with management discussion and analysis, industry reports, and other data to determine the future revenues of the firm.

Let's say a firm has more inventory on hand. It can be related to an increase in demand, so the firm is collecting more inventory. If sales are reduced with an increase in inventory and finished goods. It can be described as a reduction in demand, and inventory can become obsolete, and there is a risk of inventory write-down.

Higher inventory turnover is good, but if it is combined with low sales growth, it means the firm is not holding adequate inventory, which can cause a further reduction in sales.

High inventory turnover may also mean that an inventory write-down has occurred, which is a sign of poor inventory management. But higher sales growth with higher inventory turnover may reflect efficiency.

Financial statement and ratio analysis of companies that use different inventory methods

Here we are to compare ratios and financial statements of companies using different inventory methods. It is very much discussed in the whole inventory section. A quick review is as follows:

Here we're going to be focusing on the effect of the choice between them when it comes to ratios.

You remember that using the weighted average cost method will land figures like cost of goods sold and inventory value somewhere in between LIFO and FIFO.

Inventory management is all about balance.

Too much inventory brings about costs like storage obsolescence or insurance. Too little inventory brings about the potential cost of experiencing a stock shortage and missing out on a sale.

We have two major ratios to look at when assessing a company's inventory management.

Inventory turnover and days inventory in hand.

You will remember these ratios from earlier in the material.

Inventory turnover = COGS/average inventory.

Days inventory on hand = 365/ inventory turnover.

From the formula for each, we can figure out why the inventory valuation method is important.

We know that the denominator of the inventory turnover formula is average inventory. With a change in the method of inventory valuation, we will experience a change in average inventory, and that would affect the ratios.

When we consider inventory in management by ratio analysis, we need to be aware of the inventory valuation method as well as the underlying business to build a meaningful comparison or evaluation.

One important factor for assessment is that these ratios have an inverse relationship.

High inventory return over means a low number of days in inventory on hand.

Lower days inventory on hand means that the company doesn't have units in its inventory for long before they are sold. That sounds great. As soon as they get stock ready for sale, it's gone.

Now, on the other hand, this might mean that the company doesn't hold enough inventory compared to what sales demand would deem appropriate, or it might mean that they have recently experienced an inventory right down.

There are a number of possibilities as to what it means to have a low number of days inventory on hand.

One ratio that is directly affected by the choice of inventory evaluation method is the gross profit margin.

Gross profit margin is given by gross profit over revenue, and since gross profit is equal to sales revenue minus cost of goods sold, a choice affecting cost of goods sold will indirectly impact gross profit and also gross profit margin.

Chapter 8: Long-lived assets

Costs that are capitalized and costs that are expensed

In long-lived assets, we have tangibles like plant and machinery, buildings, tools, etc., and intangible assets like goodwill, patents, etc.

In this section, we need to distinguish between the costs that are capitalized and the costs that are expensed related to acquiring long-lived assets.

The basic rule is simple. Any expenditure that is expected to provide a future economic benefit over multiple periods must be capitalized. Capitalized costs are recorded in the balance sheet at the purchasing price or fair value.

When an expenditure is not expected to provide a future economic benefit over multiple periods, it should be expensed in the current period. These are recorded on the income statement and are counted with operating cash flows.

There are various types of costs that're expected to provide multiple years of economic benefit. For example, if a major part of the machine is replaced. The cost of that part should be capitalized because it would be expected to provide multiple years of economic benefit.

Anything that extends the useful life of an asset should be capitalized.

On the other hand, training costs or costs for regular maintenance would be examples of costs that will not provide multiple periods of economic benefit. These kinds of costs must be expensed in the current period, and you will be expected to be able to discern between these types of costs and understand which should be capitalized and which should be expensed.

Financial reporting of the following types of intangible assets: Purchased, internally developed, and acquired in a business combination.

Intangible assets are assets that do not bear a physical substance.

They are of two types.   Identifiable assets   and unidentifiable assets.

Identifiable intangible: These are assets that represent a contractual or legal right that can be separated from the owning entity under expected to generate a future economic benefit.

These assets might include.
- Patents.
- Copyrights.
- Brand recognition or a trademark.

An unidentifiable intangible asset is an asset that bears no physical substance, and it does not match the criteria of identifiable intangible assets.

One good example of an unidentifiable intangible asset is goodwill, the excessive purchase price over the fair value of assets acquired.

There are two other broad categories of intangible assets.
- Assets with finite lives
- Assets with indefinite life

An asset with a finite life must be amortized (Similar to a tangible asset). Whereas the cost of an asset with an indefinite life will not be amortized but will be tested annually for impairment.

If impairment occurs, then the asset's value will be written down on the balance sheet and the firm will report a loss on its income statement.

Accounting for intangibles depends on how they were acquired.

- Assets might be purchased.
- Developed internally.
- Or acquired as part of the business combination.

When an asset is purchased, the accounting treatment is quite similar to tangible long-lived assets.

The purchase price is assumed to be equal to fair value, and that's the figure used to record the asset on the balance sheet. Then

For assets that were developed internally, the accounting treatment is a bit different.

When an asset is purchased, the company will have one easily identifiable transaction that can drive an asset being capitalized on the balance sheet.

Assets that are developed internally will have come about through a series of expenses the company would have recognized in the periods in which they were incurred. The company will have spent money over time on a wide variety of expenses, and it's the combination of all of these varying expenses that leads the company to own this intangible asset. So, the company will recognize a series of expenditures on its income statement over time. These together will develop into an intangible asset that they own.

A good example would be continuous expenditures on an R&D program or an advertising or marketing plan.

Over time, these might develop into a recognizable brand and brand recognition.

The differing accounting treatments we have seen here will spark a major difference between the financial statements of companies that purchase assets and those that have developed them internally.

On the one hand, you have companies with assets on the balance sheet compared to companies that do not have assets to report. This is because companies that develop their assets internally have expensed their acquisition costs as they were being developed.

At the same time, you have these purchasing companies recognizing expenditures as investing cash flows. While the companies developing the assets are recognizing these expenses as operating cash flows.

Intangibles acquired as part of the business combination: Assets acquired through a business combination are accounted for using the acquisition method. Assets acquired are recorded on the balance sheet of the acquirer at fair value. The difference between the overall purchase price and the combined amount attributable to the acquired assets is recorded as goodwill.

It's important to know that this is what we consider goodwill to be an identifiable intangible asset. It cannot be separated from the acquired business.

How capitalizing versus expensing costs affects financial statements and ratios

When the cost is capitalized or expensed, the choice affects net income, shareholders' equity, total assets, cash flow from operations, and cash flow from investing and financial ratios. Let's see how it affects

Net income:
When a firm chooses to capitalize expenditure, it postpones the recognition of an expense in the income statement. So, the firm will report higher net income. But in the coming years, when the capitalized expense is reported in the income statement in the process of amortization or depreciation, the firm will report lower net income.

However, the total net income remains the same under both the techniques over the lifetime of the asset. Since both capitalizing and expensing have different effects on the financial statements, an analyst should adjust the numbers for a better comparison.

Shareholders' Equity
We know that capitalization gives us higher net income. It also increases shareholders' equity as retained earnings are greater. As capitalizing results in asset creation, total assets increased, but liabilities are unaffected. When the cost is to be allocated to the income statement in the coming years, net income, retained earnings, and shareholders' equity will be reduced.

If the firm chooses to expense, retained earnings and shareholders' equity will be decreased in those periods.

Cash Flow Statement: When we capitalize expenditure, it goes into the cash flow statement under cash flow from investing activities as an outflow. On the other hand, if the expenditure is an expense, it goes into cash flow from operations as an outflow. It means capitalizing gives us higher cash flow from operations and less cash flow from investing activities. And expensing an expenditure gives us lower cash flow from operations and higher cash flow from investing activities. If we assume there is no tax difference, the total of the cash flow statement remains the same.

Financial Ratios: When we capitalize an expenditure, we are actually increasing total assets and equity (in the current period). So, the ratios in which total assets or equity are in the denominator, like debt to assets and debt to equity, are lower. And of course, ratios with total assets or equity in the numerator are higher, like ROA, ROE. In subsequent periods, the ROA and ROE will be lower as we have to depreciate the capitalized expense.

When a firm recognizes an expenditure as an expense, in the first period, net income, Total assets, and equity will decrease. So, the ratios like ROE and ROA will be lower. In subsequent periods, these ratios will be higher. An analyst must be very careful in judging firms.

If a firm buys an asset with a loan and pays interest. The firm can capitalize that interest expenditure. By capitalizing interest expenditure, the total interest expense goes down. So, the interest coverage ratio (EBIT/interest expense), which measures a firm's ability to meet interest expense, will be higher (which is a good sign). So, a firm that decided to expense interest expenditure comes up with a lower interest coverage ratio. An analyst must calculate the interest coverage ratio by using total interest expenditure (including capitalized interest). So, this is considered to be a better measure, and bond rating companies often use this method.

Different depreciation methods for property, plant, and equipment and how they affect depreciation expense, financial statements, and ratios.

Different depreciation methods for property, plant, and equipment

We have three methods.
- Straight line
- Accelerated
- Units of production.

Straight-line method: In this method, we allocate an equal amount of the asset's value to each year of its depreciable life (useful life).

We take the cost of the asset minus salvage value and divide by the number of years. Formula

Depreciation per year = {Cost of asset- salvage value}/ number of useful years

Accelerated method: It is used when a greater proportion of the asset's cost is allocated to the earlier years of its useful life. This method is more appropriate in cases where the actual usage of the asset is greater in its earlier years.

One commonly used accelerated depreciation method is the double declining balance method.

Under this system, two things can change compared to the straight-line method.

First, we use an acceleration factor of two on the left to increase the proportion of the assets valued appreciated in the early years.

And second, instead of handling the salvage value here in the calculation of the expense amount, we account for the accumulated depreciation as we progress through time. We will handle salvage value by stopping the depreciation process when the asset's carrying value (historical cost less accumulated depreciation) reaches that salvage value. The formula is as under

Depreciation for a period = 2 x straight-line

Units of production method: In this system, the asset's value is allocated based on the actual usage of the asset in a particular period, rather than trying to model the usage of the asset over its useful life.

When we model the usage of the asset over its useful life, a company will be paying much closer attention to the actual usage of the asset, and depreciation is based on a much closer reflection of reality.

Depreciation for a year

$$= \frac{cost - salvage\ value}{life\ ife\ in\ output\ units} * output\ units\ in\ that\ period$$

Component depreciation: IFRS requires the depreciation of an asset in components. For example, a building has components of walls, Roof, etc., and furniture has tables, chairs, etc. Each of these components can be depreciated separately. In US GAAP, we do not use component depreciation

Effects: Now we need to describe the effect of the choice of depreciation method on the financial statements and ratios.

The choice of depreciation method affects the company's reported assets through changes in the asset's carrying values. They are affecting operating income through the amount of the depreciation expense, and their net income through the depreciation expense.

This in turn, will affect any ratios that use those figures, like

Fixed asset turnover, Total asset turnover, operating profit margin, operating return on assets, and return on assets.

Now, from the formula for the straight-line method, we can see that the depreciation expense is inversely related to both useful life and salvage value.

If the company assumes a longer useful life, then the depreciation expense comes down. And if the company assumes a higher salvage value depreciation expense comes down.

For this section, we need to be aware of the fact that companies will sometimes use the useful life and residual value of an asset to manipulate a depreciation schedule and an indirect consequence of that is to manipulate earnings.

Remember that longer useful lives and higher residual values bring down the depreciation expense, which will mean a higher income.

Calculation of depreciation has been covered in the reading on expense recognition on the income statement.

Different amortization methods for intangible assets with finite lives, and how the choice of amortization method and assumptions affect amortization expense, financial statements, and ratios

Here we are only considering intangibles with finite lives here. We're not going to test goodwill for impairment right now.

When we are calculating amortization for intangibles that have finite lives, the methods (of amortization) are exactly the same as the depreciation of tangible assets.

Straight line, accelerated, and units of production: It's all about allocating the cost of the asset to the years of its useful life.

Calculation of amortization expense
Let`s say Company A acquired another company and now they report some intangible assets on their book as follows.

Intangible assets	value	Useful life
Patent	$800000	5 years
Copyright	$300000	0 (with $10000 ɘsidual value)
Good will	$100000	

Using the straight-line method, calculate the total carrying value of the company`s intangible assets at the end of the year.

We know the straight line amortization (also depreciation) formula.

Amortization expense $for\ each\ year$

$$= ((Cost - \text{salvage or residual value}))/(\text{useful life.})$$

For patent, we have a cost of 800000 and 5 5-year useful life, and we have not been given a residual value, so plugging that information into the formula, we get

$$\frac{(800000 - 0)}{5} = 160000$$

With copyright, we have a cost of 300000, a 10-year useful life, and a residual value of 10000. Again, plugging into the formula, we come up with an amortization expense

$$\frac{(300000 - 10000)}{10} = 29000$$

Remember that goodwill is an intangible asset with indefinite useful life, so there won't be any amortization charge. We only amortize intangible assets that have finite useful lives.

Intangible assets	value	Amortization expense
Patent	$800000	160000
Copyright	$300000	29000
Good will	$100000	
Total amortization expense for the period		189000
Intangibles at end of period	800000+300000+)000 -189000 =1011000	

The effect of the choice of amortization method on the financial statements:

Through changes in carrying values and amortization expenses, the company will see an impact on assets, income, and ratios depending on the method of amortization chosen.

Describe the effects of assumptions concerning useful life and residual value on amortization expense.

Again, an important point here is that the inverse relationship exists between the expense and useful life and residual value. Longer lives mean higher residual values, which would equate to the company recognizing a lower amortization expense in the period.

Revaluation model

The revaluation model is a simple system, rarely used in practice, for reporting the value of a firm's assets. This is only allowed under IFRS. Under U. S. GAAP, companies must report their balance sheet assets using the historical cost model.

This model is opposite to the historical cost model. (In the historical cost model, we report original cost minus accumulated depreciation amount on the balance sheet along with the depreciation expense on the income statement), In the revaluation model, we report the assets on the balance sheet at fair value and post a gradual decline in fair value as losses to the income statement.

Following are the conditions must be fulfilled in order to use this model

- An active market must exist for the asset. Without an active market in place, reliable estimates of fair value would be impossible to obtain.
- Firms must be using similar methods of reporting for similar assets. It means they cannot pick and choose certain assets to report under the historical cost model and then others to report using the revaluation model.
- Assets are written down in value with usage and age as the fair value declines. As the asset`s value in the active market changes, so should the reported value change.

Note: if the value of the asset increases in the market and that increase goes beyond the asset`s initial cost, that gain should be reported as a revaluation surplus with shareholders' equity and not as a gain on the income statement.

Impairment of property, plant, and equipment and intangible assets

Depreciation and amortization are scheduled models for the decline in asset value over its useful life; impairment is reserved for a decline in the asset value at a particular point in time that was not anticipated.

The first major point we need to make here is that a company will only test the value of an asset for impairment if there is an indication that an impairment may have occurred (may be due to some incident like obsolescence, A decline in demand, or a technological advancement).
Remember that we need a reason to test for impairment.

Under IFRS, testing for impairment means looking at the difference between an asset's carrying value and its recoverable value.

Carrying value = asset's original cost - accumulated depreciation - any previous impairments or reversals. It is the currently reported value of the asset.

Recoverable value is either the asset's fair value less any costs that would have to be incurred to sell it or the asset's value in use, whichever is higher.

Value in use is the present value of the asset's expected future cash flows if usage continued.

So, under IFRS, we have an impaired asset if the carrying value is greater than the recoverable value. When that occurs, the company must write down or decrease the value of the asset as recorded on its balance sheet. And they would record a loss equal to that change in value on their income statement.
Note that an impairment loss is a non-cash amount, so the cash flow statement will not see any impact.

Under U. S. GAAP, we impair an asset if the carrying value is greater than the fair value.

It means the company will only write down the asset's value and post a loss to the income statement if the asset's carrying value is deemed to be not recoverable. So even if fair value is actually less than the asset's current carrying value, a write-down will only be recorded if the asset's carrying value is also below the sum of its expected future cash flows.

This isn't the same thing as value in use from IFRS. Value in use is an IFRS measure.

With US GAAP, we're comparing carrying value to both fair value and the undiscounted sum of the asset's expected future cash flows.

Following the write-down, if an asset's value increases, companies reporting with IFRS may report an impairment reversal. They can increase the value of the asset on their reports to reflect that increase in value, even after they have posted a loss for a prior decline in value.

U. S. GAAP does not allow for impairment reversals.

De-recognition of property, plant and equipment and intangible assets

Derecognition is the process by which a company removes an asset from its financial statements.

There are three situations in which an asset will be derecognized.

- When the asset is sold.
- Exchanged.
- Or abandoned.

When an asset is sold, the difference between the sale proceeds and the asset's carrying value will go into the income statement either as a gain or as a loss. That same figure will also need to be recognized on the cash flow statement as an investing cash inflow.

If an old asset is exchanged for a newer one we will be removing the carrying value of the old asset from the balance sheet and adding the fair value of the new asset as well as that a gain or loss will hit the income statement to reflect the difference between the fair value of the new asset and the carrying value of the old asset.

If an asset is abandoned or retired, The treatment is very similar to a sale, only in this case, there will be no sale proceeds. There will be a loss to the income statement, and since no cash changes hands, the cash flow statement will not be affected.

How impairment, revaluation, and derecognition of property, plant, and equipment and intangible assets affect financial statements and ratios

Impairment: Impairment reduces the value of an asset (tangible and intangible). We record it as a loss in the income statement; reduce it from retained earnings (equity) and assets. So, the Return on Assets (ROA) and Return on Equity (ROE) ratios are lower as net income declined. In the coming years, as we have impaired the asset's value, the depreciation expense will be less. So, the net income would be higher (than that if the asset were not impaired), so would the ROA and ROE. The asset turnover ratio would be higher in the impairment year and subsequent years as the asset's value is lower now. As the impairment is a non-cash loss, there would be no effect on the cash flow statement.

Analysis of impairment: when a company impairs its assets, that means the management failed to depreciate or amortize the asset according to the market conditions. It also means that they were recognizing less expense and more income in previous years. Recognition of impairment can be a good opportunity for management to manipulate earnings and ROE, ROA, etc. Sometimes, management decides not to recognize the impairment loss until the year of good earnings to show a smooth income pattern. On the other hand, early impairment loss could be done by management to show higher income and ROE, ROA in the coming years. A good level of judgment from the analyst is required to understand the reason behind the impairment.

Revaluation: US GAAP mostly does not allow revaluation. We only record long-lived assets as cost minus depreciation, less any impairment. One exception to this rule is for long-lived assets held for sale. In this case, the previous impairment can be reversed.

Under IFRS, we can use the revaluation method and reverse impairment. IFRS allows us to use the revaluation model for some assets and the cost model for others.

Revaluation has the following effects:

- It increases the asset's value, so the equity increases.
- It lowers leverage ratios, i.e., debt to total assets and debt to total equity (as the denominator increases).
- When an asset's value increases, then the depreciation expense also increases (as we calculate depreciation as a percentage of the asset's value). So, the net income decreases.
- ROA and ROE decrease as the numerator decreases and the denominator increases.

Analysis for revaluation: Analysts must check the reason behind the revaluation because it can also be a good opportunity for management to manipulate results. He/ she must look for industry overview and market conditions for the asset's value.

De-recognition of Assets: De-recognition is the process by which a company removes an asset from its financial statements.

There are three situations in which an asset will be derecognized.

- When the asset is sold.
- Exchanged.
- Or abandoned.

When an asset is sold, the difference between the sale proceeds and the asset's carrying value will go into the income statement either as a gain or as a loss. That same figure will also need to be recognized on the cash flow statement as an investing cash inflow.

If an old asset is exchanged for a newer one we will be removing the carrying value of the old asset from the balance sheet and adding the fair value of the new asset as well as that a gain or loss will hit the income statement to reflect the difference between the fair value of the new asset and the carrying value of the old asset.

If an asset is abandoned or retired, the treatment is very similar to a sale, only in this case, there will be no sale proceeds. There will be a loss to the income statement, and since no cash changes hands, the cash flow statement will not be affected.

Financial statement presentation of and disclosures relating to property, plant, and equipment, and intangible assets

For companies reporting under IFRS, each of the following items must be disclosed for property, plant, and equipment.
- The basis for measuring the asset's value (i.e., historical cost, etc.),
- Depreciation method and depreciation rate used,
- Gross carrying value of asset, a reconciliation of any change in the asset's carrying value over the period,
- Any restrictions related to the assets that are pledged as collateral and any agreements that are currently in place for the future acquisition of assets.

For intangible assets, all the above disclosures plus a disclosure of whether the intangible asset's useful life is finite or indefinite are required.

For impaired assets, we need to disclose
- The amounts of any impairment write-downs or reversals.
- Impacts of those write-downs and reversals on the income statement
- Circumstances that brought about that impairment or reversal.

For investment property, disclosures depend on the valuation method used. We will discuss this later on, but in terms of disclosures, firms that report under the cost model would follow the same guidelines as ordinary long-lived assets. Firms reporting using the fair value model will be required to include additional disclosures related to the determination of fair value.

Under U. S. GAAP, the disclosure requirements are not as detailed. Companies must disclose the aggregate depreciation expense for the period, classified carrying values of the major depreciable asset classes, and a general description of the depreciation method used.

For intangible assets, a company will have similar disclosure requirements, such as aggregate amortization expense amount, Classified listing of growth carrying amounts, classified accumulated amortization figures, and the estimate for the expected amortization expense for the next five years.

Companies reporting under U. S. GAAP do not have the option of reversing impairments.

For impaired assets, the following disclosures are required under U. S. GAAP
- a description of the impaired assets,
- the circumstances that led to the impairment,
- the method used to determine the asset`s fair value,
- The amount of the impairment loss and its impact on the income statement.

Analysis of financial statement disclosures regarding property, plant, and equipment and intangible assets

Financial statement disclosures regarding property, plant, and equipment are helpful for an analyst to understand the company`s fixed assets and the choice of depreciation and or amortization taken. One of the most common metrics used by analysts from this information is to calculate the average age of an asset. Average age calculation has two benefits:

- The average useful life gives us the timing of future capital expenditure and financing requirements of the firm.
- To estimate if the older asset might be giving the owning entity a comparative disadvantage.

The following are some useful calculations for an analyst:

Average age of assets in years $= \dfrac{Accumulated\ depreciation}{current\ year\ depreciation\ expense}$, This calculation is more accurate in firms using straight line depreciation method. The answer is highly dependent on the types of assets used.

Total useful life of asset in years $= \dfrac{Historical\ cost}{annual\ depreciation\ expense}$,

We know that historical cost is the cost of the asset before deduction of any depreciation.

Remaining useful life (in years) $= \dfrac{Ending\ net\ balance\ of\ PP\&E}{Annual\ depriciation}$, we know ending net PP&E = Gross PP&E – Accumulated depreciation

The remaining useful life can also be calculated as average depreciable life - average age

Annual capital expenditures to depreciation expense ratio: another common measure used by analysts to determine whether the firm is replacing its PP&E at the same rate as its assets are being depreciated.

Financial reporting of investment property vs property, plant, and equipment

In this section, we are required to differentiate between the reporting of investment property and the property, plant, and equipment.

Remember, this only applies to companies reporting under IFRS. U. S. GAAP does not distinguish between investment property and other long-lived assets.

Under IFRS, Investment property must be valued using either the cost model or the fair value model. But whatever we have decided, we have to stick with it for all investment properties. We can't decide on asset-by-asset basis which model to work with.

The cost model we've seen before with other long-lived assets. And for investment properties, there is no difference in the accounting treatment.

The fair value model is different from the revaluation model we looked at earlier in this section.

The revaluation model required us to post certain types of asset value increases to shareholders' equity in an account called the revaluation surplus. The fair value model requires that we post any gains directly to the income statement.

One final thing to consider here is the accounting treatment of transferring an asset between classifications.

What do we do if we want to reclassify an asset from investment property to PP&E or vice versa? If we currently hold the asset as part of PP&E using the fair value method, we treat the transfer like a revaluation. So, the reported value of PP&E is the fair value on the day of revaluation, less any subsequent accumulated depreciation. For assets transferred from investment property to PP&E, we take the asset's fair value at

the time of transfer and use that as the asset`s cost basis for
future reporting as part of PP&E.

Chapter 9: Income Tax

Accounting profit, taxable income, deferred tax assets, deferred tax liabilities, valuation allowance, taxes payable, and income tax expense.

Most of the time, income tax rules are different than financial statement rules. So, the income tax payable (from the perspective of income tax authorities) may be different from what is recognized in the income statement.

Some most common terminologies of income tax

Taxable income: *It is* the base income on which *the income tax authorities impose* tax. It is the income on which the tax is deductible by law.

Taxes payable: it is the liability that arises from taxable income. It is the current tax expense calculated from taxable income according to the tax laws.

Income tax paid: It is the actual outflow from income as tax expense.

Tax loss carried forward: it is the current or past losses that can be used to reduce taxable income (and current tax payable) in the future. It causes deferred tax liability.

Tax base: The Amount of an asset or liability used for tax calculation and reporting purposes.

Financial reporting terminologies related to income tax:

Accounting profit is also called income before tax or earnings before tax. This is pre-tax income calculated according to the financial accounting standards.

Income tax expense: Income tax expense = taxes payable + changes in deferred tax liabilities − changes in deferred tax assets. It is the income tax recognized in financial statements (income tax and any changes in deferred tax liabilities and assets)

Deferred tax liabilities: This is a balance sheet item. It shows any excess of income tax expense over income taxes payable. It is expected to be paid in the future. A very good example for this is when a company chose to use accelerated depreciation for tax purposes but uses the straight line method for financial reporting. Using the accelerated depreciation method, the depreciation expense will be higher in the first period, and the tax payable will be less. Of course, the tax payable would be higher in later periods. For this company, it chooses to recognize higher tax payable in the first period, so the effect will be offset in the coming years.

Deferred tax assets: This is a balance sheet item. It shows any excess of income tax payable over income tax expense. It is expected to be recovered in the future. When this happens, we carry forward the tax loss.

Valuation allowance: When a deferred tax asset is not likely to be realized, we reduce the asset. That reduction is called a valuation allowance.

Carrying value: Net balance sheet value of an asset or liability.

Permanent difference: A difference between taxable income (tax return) and pretax income unlikely to reverse in the future.

Temporary difference: This is a difference between the tax base of an asset/liability and the carrying value of an asset/liability that will result in either a higher or lower tax amount in the current period. This difference would offset in the future, that's why it is called a temporary difference. The examples of this will come after a little bit in this section.

Creation of deferred tax liabilities and assets, their treatment, and other factors

Normally, the treatment of accounting items is different for tax reporting and financial reporting. This difference is due to the following reasons

- The timing of revenue recognition is different for financial reporting than for tax purposes.
- Some gains and or losses have a difference in recognition for both.
- Some revenues are to be recognized in financial statements but cannot be recognized for tax returns, and vice versa.
- Some assets and liabilities have different carrying values for tax and financial reporting purposes.
- Some financial statement adjustments may not be recognized or adjusted in the tax base of those items.
- Some tax losses from the past can reduce future tax returns.

Deferred tax liability: When income tax expense is greater than taxes payable due to temporary differences, the deferred tax liability is created (it has to be paid in the future). It can be caused by the following reasons:

- Revenues and or gains are recognized in the income statement but not yet included on the tax return due to temporary differences.
- Expenses and or losses are used to tax deduction but are not recognized in the income statement.

A most common cause of deferred tax liability is when an accelerated depreciation method is used on the tax purposes, but the straight-line depreciation method is used in the income statement.

Deferred Tax Assets: When taxes payable are greater than income tax expense (in the income statement) due to temporary differences, a deferred tax asset is created. The following reasons can cause deferred tax asset creation:

- Revenues and or gains are not yet recognized in the income Statement but are used for tax purposes.
- Expenses and or losses are recognized in the income statement but not yet used for tax deduction.
- Carried forward losses reduce future taxable income.

Tax loss carry forwards are used to reduce future taxable income.

Treatment for Analytical Purposes
If deferred tax liabilities are to reverse in the future, they should be treated as liabilities (for analysis). If not, they must be classified as equity

The analyst has to decide when and why we should treat them as liability or equity on a case-by-case basis.

Tax base of a company's assets and liabilities

Tax Base of Assets: This is the value attributed to an asset for tax purposes. If that asset is sold, that amount (tax base) is tax-deductible.

Carrying value of asset: It is the net value of an asset reported in financial statements. Carrying value of asset = Cost of asset – accumulated depreciation or amortization – any impairment if occurred.

Calculation of the tax base of assets

Accounts receivable: Let`s say a firm has receivables of $ 10000. As the collection is uncertain, the firm recognizes the bad debts reserve of $1ooo. But tax authorities do not recognize bad debt reserve unless it actually occurred (they seem worthless). At the end of one year, the tax base is $10000, but the carrying value is $9000 (10000-1000). So, the deferred tax asset is created. When the bad debts are not collectable in the second period, they would be tax-deductible.

Depreciable equipment: Let`s say the cost of the equipment is $5000. The firm recognizes depreciation expense of $500 in the income statement for 10 years. For tax purposes, the asset is depreciated at $1000 per year for five years. After the end of the first period (year), the tax base of the asset is $4000 (5000-1000) while the carrying value of the asset is 5000-500 =$4500. An account of deferred tax liability ($1,000 × tax rate) is created to adjust the timing difference of financial reporting and tax depreciation calculation.

Tax Base of Liabilities: Tax base of a liability = Liability's carrying value - amounts deductible on the tax return in the future.

Calculation of the tax base of liabilities

Advance payment by customer: Let`s say, a customer bought goods for $1000 from our firm and paid in advance. The goods have to be shipped next year. For taxation purposes revenues received in advance are taxable. But for our firm $1000 is a liability. The carrying value of this liability is $1000. Next year, when we ship the goods, this liability will be removed.

We know that the tax base of a liability = carrying value of the liability - any amounts that will be deductible on the tax return in the future.

The advance is already taxed and will not be taxable in the future; the tax base of this liability is zero now ($1000 -$1000). As we have paid tax on $1000 but have not yet reported it on the income statement, and it will cause a future deduction in tax, a deferred tax asset is created.

Delay in expense recognition: Some expenses, like Warranties, are recognized in the income statement, but for tax return, they are only tax deductible when actually expensed. If, for example, a firm estimates that $1000 of warranty expense is required for next year for the goods sold this year. The tax authorities do not allow for the deduction of warranties unless it is actually performed. The carrying value of warranty liability is $1000. The tax base = carrying value – any amount deductible in the future. So, the 1000 – 1000 = 0 is the tax base. In this case, the expense is recognized in delay. So, a deferred tax asset is created.

Note payable. Notes payable are treated for tax and income statements alike. So, no deferred asset or liability is created in this case as there is no delayed or early recognition of expense.

Calculation and interpretation of income tax expense, income taxes payable, deferred tax assets, deferred tax liabilities, and adjustments to the financial statements related to a change in the income tax rate

Deferred tax liability: Let`s say an asset`s original cost is $100000. The depreciation method for tax purposes is the accelerated depreciation method. The depreciation expense using this method is 40000, 30000, 20000, and 10000 for years 1, 2, 3, and 4, respectively. While the firm is using the straight line method for financial reporting, the following table shows income statement items for financial purposes (using the straight line method at a 25% depreciation rate). The tax rate is 20%.

	YEAR 1	year 2	year 3	year 4	year 1-4
EBITDA	700000	700000	700000	700000	2800000
Depreciation (SL)	25000	25000	25000	25000	100000
Pre tax income	675000	675000	675000	675000	2700000
Tax rate	20%	20%	20%	20%	20%
Tax payable	135000	135000	135000	135000	540000
Income after tax	540000	540000	540000	540000	2160000

The following table shows income statement items by using accelerated method

EBITDA	700000	700000	700000	700000	2800000
Depreciation (AR)	40000	30000	20000	10000	100000
Pre tax income	660000	670000	680000	690000	2700000
Tax rate	20%	20%	20%	20%	20%
Tax payable	132000	134000	136000	138000	540000
Income after tax	528000	536000	544000	552000	2160000

In year 1, the firm recognized an income tax expense of $135000, but they actually paid $132000 on their tax return. So, a difference of 3000 is recorded in the balance sheet as deferred tax liability because the income tax expense is higher than the actual tax paid. We can calculate deferred tax liability from income tax expense and tax return (tax payable). At the end of the first year, the carrying value of the asset is 75000 (i.e., 100000-25000), but the tax base of the asset is 60000 (i.e., 100000- 40000). The difference between the asset`s carrying value and tax base is 15000. We multiply the difference by the tax rate (15000 x .20), we get 3000 DTL.

In year two, the tax expense is 135000, but the tax return is 134000. 1000 difference would go into the balance sheet as dtl (added in the previous balance). So, the tax expense for year 2 is the tax return plus any change in dtl. Which is 134000 + 1000 = 135000. In year 3, the tax expense is still 135000, but the tax return is 136000. So, the tax expense for year 3 would be tax return + change in dtl. We are paying 1000 more than our income tax expense, so tax expense would be 136000 + (-1000)

= 135000. In year 4, all the dtl would reverse, and we would end up paying the same total income tax expense as if we used the same depreciation methods for both (financial reporting and tax return).

Deferred tax Asset: Now, if we invert the above-mentioned examples, we can understand deferred tax asset. Using the same example in another way, let's just say the accelerated depreciation method is used for financial reporting, while for tax returns, we use the straight line depreciation method. All the other data remains the same. At the end of the first year, the tax payable is 132000, while the tax return is 135000. Since this difference is temporary, a deferred tax asset is created. In the second year, the tax payable is 134000, but the tax return is 135000 again. This again adds up to the deferred tax asset. In the third year, the tax expense is 136000, and the tax return is 135000, which reverses the deferred tax asset. At the end of year 4, all the DTAs are reversed, and we end up paying the same total tax return.

Effect of tax rate changes on a company's financial statements and ratios

A change in tax rate changes the DTA and DTL. An increase (decrease) in tax rate will increase (decrease) DTA and DTL. Changes in DTA and DTL will affect the income tax expense for the current period.
As we know that;
Income tax expense = taxes payable + ΔDTL $-\Delta$DTA

Let's use the previous example. What would happen if the tax rate changed from 20% to 30%? We know that the tax base of the asset in year 1 is 100000-40000 = 60000, while the carrying value is 75000. The difference is 15000. Previously, the

DTL was 15000x 20% = 3000. With a change in tax rate new DTL would be 15000 x 30% = 4500.

AS DTA and DTL are balance sheet items, any ratio that comes up with assets or liabilities would be affected by changes in DTA and DTL.

Temporary and permanent differences in pre-tax accounting income and taxable income

Temporary difference: A temporary difference between pre-tax accounting income and taxable income is a difference that will reverse in the future. Temporary difference creates a deferred tax asset or a deferred tax liability. It happens due to the timing difference of revenues and or expense recognition in tax rules and accounting rules. Tax rules may recognize an expense later than accounting rules, or tax rules may recognize income earlier than accounting rules.
Temporary difference can be of two types

Taxable temporary difference: This results in future taxable income. In this case, we create deferred tax liability.

Deductible temporary difference: This results in future tax deductions. In this case, we had created a deferred tax asset.

Permanent difference: A permanent difference is a difference between taxable income and pretax accounting income that will not reverse in the future. So, it does not create deferred tax assets or deferred tax liabilities. Permanent difference may be a result of an untaxable revenue or a non-deductible expense. It can also be a result of a tax credit. Permanent difference can create a difference between a firm`s effective tax rate and its statutory tax rate.

Statutory tax rate: It is the tax rate of the jurisdiction where the firm operates.

Effective tax rate: It is derived from the formula,

$$Effective\ tax\ rate = \frac{income\ tax\ expense}{pre\ tax\ accountin\ income}$$

Valuation allowance for deferred tax assets

We know that deferred tax assets are created from temporary differences that would reverse in the future.

According to US GAAP, if there are more than 50 % chances that the deferred tax asset will not reverse fully or partially in the future due to insufficient taxable income, a valuation account is created (valuation allowance is only created for DTA).

Valuation account is a contra account that reduces the net balance sheet DTA, and reduces net income (by increasing income tax expense). If in subsequent periods the circumstances changed, the valuation allowance can be decreased to increase DTA (which will increase net income).

It is up to management to use a valuation allowance. If they are earning sufficient income valuation allowance is not required. But if they have a history of inadequate earnings (so, they could not carry forward income tax losses), they should maintain a valuation allowance.

We know that increasing valuation allowance reduces net income and vice versa; management can manipulate earnings by using this allowance. Whenever a company reports huge DTA (and or valuation allowance), the analyst must review the firm`s performance to judge whether they are going to realize

DFA or not. Analysts must also analyze that a huge change in valuation allowance must be economically justified.

Under IFRS, no valuation allowance is maintained. We only reduce or increase DTA directly.

Recognition and measurement of current and deferred tax items

- Current tax payables or recoverables depend upon the current tax rate.
- The deferred tax assets and liabilities are created due to temporary differences. Their measurement depends upon the future tax rate when the difference is going to reverse or deferred tax items are going to settle.
- All the deferred tax items (assets and liabilities) must be reassessed and measured according to their probable future economic benefits. For example, if the future taxable income is expected to be lower than the DTA, the liability must be adjusted accordingly.
- If deferred tax liability is expected not to reverse in the future, it must be treated as equity by the analyst. (DTL is not going to reverse for any reason).
- If there is uncertainty in tax payments (timing of payment and amount of tax) analyst should exclude DTL from analysis (do not consider it as liability or equity).

Disclosures relating to deferred tax items and the effective tax rate reconciliation, and their effects on a company's financial statements and financial ratios

Disclosure: The Following information is required to be disclosed relating to deferred tax items,
- Deferred tax assets and liabilities, valuation allowance, and net change in valuation allowance over time.

- Unrecognized deferred tax liability (if any) for undistributed earnings.
- Effect of current year tax on temporary difference (and on DTA, DTL).
- Components of income tax expense.
- Reconciliation of reported income tax expense and the tax expense based.
- Tax losses carry forwards.

Analysis of effective tax rate reconciliation

Sometimes, the reported income tax expense is different from the amount based on the statutory income tax rate. We know that the statutory tax rate is the tax rate that is imposed by law in that area. The following could be the reasons for those differences.
- Difference in tax rate in different jurisdictions.
- Permanent tax differences like tax exemptions, tax credits, non-deductible expenses, and the difference between operating income and capital gains.
- Changes in tax laws of the jurisdictions in which the firm or its subsidiary operates.
- Deferred tax assets arise from reinvestment of earnings of foreign and domestic affiliates.
- Tax holidays

An analyst has to understand each of these reconciliation items, their impact on future earnings, their past changes, and expected future changes in these elements.

It's also important for an analyst to include only those items in her analysis that are continuous in nature. For example, different tax rates in different states (or countries), income exempted from tax, tax credits, and non-deductible expenses are continuous in nature. While tax holidays and capital gain taxes are periodic. The footnotes and MD&A should be reviewed to understand the nature of an item.

Income tax accounting under International Financial Reporting Standards (IFRS) and US generally accepted accounting principles (GAAP)

Accounting treatment of income tax under US GAAP and IFRS is mostly similar. The differences are stated as under,

Upward Revaluation: Under US GAAP, upward revaluation is not allowed.

Under IFRS, upward is permitted and results in equity.

Valuation allowance: Under US GAAP, we maintain a valuation allowance to offset any reduction in DTA.

Under IFRS, we directly reduce DTA (no valuation allowance is needed).

Classification: Under US GAAP, the classification depends on the underlying asset or liability.

Under IFRS, we classify DTA and DTL as non-current

Chapter 10: Non-current or long-term Liabilities

Some terminologies first

Bond: A Bond is a debt instrument. It is a contractual promise between two parties. One is the issuer of the bond (borrower). The other party is the lender (bondholder). The bondholder obligates the issuer to make payments (interest and principal) to the bondholder over the terms of the bond (until maturity). Usually, this contract has two types of payments: 1. periodic interest payment, 2. Principal amount payment at maturity

Some terminologies related to the bond

Face value: It is the value of the principal amount repaid to the bondholder at maturity, also called par value. This value is used to calculate the coupon payment.

Coupon rate: the interest rate stated on the bond.

Coupon payment: the amount of interest periodic interest payments to the bondholder. It is calculated as follows,

Coupon payment = face value x coupon rate.

Effective rate of interest: It is the rate of interest that equates the present value of the future cash flows of the bond (interest + principal) to the issue price. (Note: issue price can be <> face value). It is the rate of interest required by bondholders to cover default, liquidity, and other risks. Coupon rate is usually fixed and stated on the bond, while the effective rate is the rate actually being received by bondholders. If a bond is issued at a discount, the effective rate is higher than the coupon rate, or if the effective rate (or market rate is higher than the coupon rate, the bond is issued at a discount, priced below par. If the market rate is equal to the coupon rate, the bond is issued at par (or priced at face value or priced at par). If the market rate is lower than the coupon rate, it means the bond is issued at a premium (priced above par).

Balance sheet liability of a bond: It is the present value of the bond`s remaining coupon payments and face value, discounted at the market rate of interest. As maturity approaches, the bond liability equalizes the face value of the bond. The value of a liability on the balance sheet is also called the book value or carrying value of the bond (or liability).

Interest expense of bond: It is calculated as, book value of the bond liability at the beginning of the period multiplied by the market rate of interest at issuance.

Initial recognition, initial measurement, and subsequent measurement of bonds

NOTE: We are going to discuss it from the issuer`s perspective.

When the bond is issued at par:

When the bond is issued at par, the yield at issuance is equal to the coupon rate of that bond. So, the present value of coupons and face value is equal to the par value. The issuance at par has the following effects on financial statements.

Income statement: On the income statement, interest expense is equal to the coupon rate.

Balance sheet: The asset (cash received from issuance) and liability (bond) increased by the face value. The book value remains the same on the balance sheet over the bond`s term.

Cash flow: On the cash flow statement, when the bond is issued, the proceeds are reported in cash flow from financing activities. Interest expense (the coupon payments) is recorded in CFO (under US GAAP) and in CFO or CFF (under IFRS) as an outflow. As the bond matures, the repayment of the principal amount is recorded in CFF as an outflow.

When the bond is issued at a discount

When the bond yield is greater than the coupon rate, it is issued at a discount. It means investors are going to pay less than the face value of the bond. It has the following effects on financial statements,

Balance sheet measurement (effects on balance sheet): In the case of discounted issuance, the balance sheet assets and liabilities are increased by the issuance proceeds of the bond. So, in the balance sheet, a discounted bond is reported at less than its face value. At any time, the book value of the bond is equal to the present value of future cash outflows (coupon and principal repayment) discounted at the bond`s yield. We use bond yield at issuance.

The difference between coupon payment and interest expense (bond yield) is the amortization of discount. In each period, amortization (increase) of discount is added to the bond liability. So, the book value of the bond and interest expense increases over time (until it reaches its face value).

When the bond is issued at a premium

When the bond`s yield <coupon payment rate, the bond is issued at a premium. It means the buyer of the bond is paying

more than the face value. It also means the proceeds received from the sale of the bond are more than the face value. Opposite to a discount bond, a premium bond is reported at more than its face value. In each period, the bond is amortized (reduced) until it reaches its face value at maturity.

Effective interest method, interest expense, amortization of bond discounts/premiums, and interest payments

There are two methods of accounting for bonds: 1. Straight line method, 2. Effective interest method

The straight line method is not allowed under IFRS. It is only allowed under US GAAP. US GAAP still does not prefer the straight-line method. So the effective interest method is a widely used method.

Straight line method: It is just like straight line depreciation method. Under this method the amortization of discount or premium is evenly distributed over the life of bond.

Effective interest method: In this method, we use the market rate of interest or bond yield at issuance (remains constant for each period of the bond). So,

Interest expense = book value of bond at issuance x bond's yield at issuance

The difference between bond yield and coupon rate is bond amortization. With effective interest method the amortization is different in each period.

The difference between coupon payment and interest expense (bond yield) is the amortization of discount. In each period, amortization (increase) of discount is added to the bond liability. So, the book value of bond and interest expense increases over time (until it reaches its face value).

When the bond`s yield <coupon payment rate, the bond is issued at premium. It means the buyer of the bond is paying more than the face value. It also means the proceeds received from the sale of the bond are more than the face value. Opposite to discount bond, a premium bond is reported at more than its face value. In each period, the bond is amortized (reduced) until it reaches its face value at maturity.

Coupon payment is a cash item, the amortization is a non-cash item, so it must be adjusted while presenting the cash flow statement.
Under US GAAP, interest paid is reported under CFO, while under IFRS, it is reported under either CFO or CFF.
Under US GAAP, a bond`s issuance cost is reported as an asset and is amortized over the bond`s life.
Under IFRS, issuance cost reduces the value of the carrying value of debt.

De-recognition of debt

There are two ways to derecognize a bond. When the bond matures or when the firm redeems the bond before maturity.
The cash paid on the maturity of the bond is reported under CFF. Once the bond is mature, no gain or loss is reported. This is because all the discount or premiums is fully amortized. It also means that at maturity, the face value is equal to the carrying value.

Sometimes a firm chooses to redeem a bond before its maturity. There are many reasons that lead toward redemption. If the interest rate falls, the firm may choose to redeem a costly bond. Other reasons may include huge earnings and or availability of other cheap financing opportunities (i.e., equity issuance). When the bond is redeemed, gain or loss is recognized as;

Book value – redemption price. If the book value is higher than the redemption price, the gain is reported and vice versa.

If the issuance cost is amortized, it must be written off and adjusted into gain or loss. If the issuance cost is adjusted into bond liability, no separate entry is needed.

A gain or loss is reported in the income statement as part of continuing operations. The analyst has to separate while forecasting the firm`s future.

In terms of the cash flow statement, the redemption price is reported under CFF. Gains or losses do not appear in the cash flow statement using the method. However, in the indirect method, gains are subtracted while loss is added to calculate CFO.

Role of debt covenants in protecting creditors.

Debt covenants: These are the restrictions imposed by the lender on the borrower to protect the lender's interests (repayment of debt).

Debt covenants reduce the default risk, so they also reduce borrowing costs. The debt covenants are of two types

    1. Affirmative covenants   2. Negative covenants

Affirmative covenants: With these covenants, the borrower promises to adhere to certain rules imposed by the lender, such as

- Maintain a certain level of assets as collateral.
- Insurance
- Timely payments of interest and principal amount, etc.

Negative covenants: With negative covenants the borrower promises to avoid certain things that might affect borrower`s ability to repay, like

- Selling certain assets
- Issuing more debt instruments
- Acquisitions.

If borrower violates any covenant, the lender can demand immediate repayment of principle amount and any outstanding interest amount.

An analyst must understand these covenants while analyzing the bond. These covenants are recoded into footnotes.

It is also important to note the extent to which these covenants restrict the issuing company while making equity analysis and the future of the company.

Financial statement presentation of and disclosures relating to debt

Firms report their long-term debt in a single line in liabilities. The current portion of long-term debt (interest payment and or the repayment of principal amount within one year) is reported in current liabilities. The details of long-term debt are disclosed under footnotes and also in management`s discussion and analysis. The footnotes are very helpful in determining the timing and amount of the payments. The footnotes normally consist following information.

Nature and Maturity of liability dates, Coated and effective interest/ market rates, Call and conversion options, Debt covenants, Assets which are pledged as security, and the amount of debt maturing in each of the next five years.

The management's discussion and analysis covers the quantitative and qualitative aspects of debt, such as obligations due and future costs of capital, respectively.

Benefits and motives for leasing assets instead of purchasing them

A leasing of assets is a contractual agreement between the lessor (owner of the asset) and the lessee (user of the asset) to use the asset for a specific time period in return for periodic payments.

Leases are of two broad types, the finance lease (in US GAAP, the Finance lease is known as a capital lease) and the operating lease.

Finance lease: In a finance lease, the lessee purchases an asset by debt (periodic payments). When both parties agree on a lease contract, the lessee records the amount as an asset and also as a liability in the balance sheet. Over the lease terms, the lessee depreciates the asset and recognizes the interest payments. This is just like purchasing of asset with borrowed money.

Operating lease: This is simply a rental agreement. No asset or liability is recorded on the balance sheet. Only rental payments (expense) are recorded in the income statement.

Benefits of leasing:
- Normally, in a lease agreement, there are no initial payments, so the leasing is less costly than purchasing the asset.

- When the lease agreement ends, the asset can be returned to the lender, so the risk of obsolescence is reduced.
- Normally, a lease agreement is more flexible than other financing modes. It can be negotiated better. So, there can be fewer restrictions.
- Operating lease is an off-balance sheet item, so the leverage ratios are better.
- In the US, a lease can be reported as a synthetic lease where the lease asset is treated as an owned asset (only for tax purposes). So, a tax reduction can be observed as depreciation and interest expenses are tax-deductible.

Financial reporting of leases from a lessee's and lessor's perspective

Lessee`s perspective:

Under IFRS, the lease can be classified as either an operating or a finance lease. The choice of classification depends upon the economic substance of the transaction. For a lease to be considered as a Finance lease (under IFRS), any of the following criteria must be met

- At the end of the lease, the title of the asset is to be transferred to the lessee.
- The lessee can purchase the asset in the future at a significantly lower price than its fair value.
- The asset is specialized and made for the lessee (only the lessee can use the asset without any significant modification)
- The lease agreement covers a major portion of the useful life of the asset.
- The present value of payments of the leased asset is significantly equal to the fair value of that asset.

US GAAP also describes some rules to classify a lease as a finance lease (in US GAAP, a Finance lease is called a capital lease. The US GAAP rules are the same as IFRS, but are considered more specific than IFRS. For US GAAP, any of the following criteria must be met for a finance lease;

- At the end of the lease, the title of the asset is to be transferred to the lessee,
- The lessee can purchase the asset in the future at a significantly lower price than its fair value.
- A *bargain purchase option* permits the lessee to purchase the asset in the future at a significantly lower price than its market fair value.
- The lease agreement covers 70% or more of the useful life of the asset.
- The present value of payments of the leased asset is 90% or more of the fair value of that asset.

If none of the above criteria is met, the lease is considered an operating lease. A lessee prefers an operating lease in general, as no asset or liability is reported in it. With a finance lease, the lessee reports assets and liabilities.

Lease to be reported by lessee:

Operating lease: No entry is made at the inception of the lease (but as discussed above, the future obligations must be disclosed under footnotes). Only rental income equal to the lease payment is recorded in the income statement as an expense. In the cash flow statement, lease payments are recorded as cash outflows under operating activities.

Finance lease: The lower of the present value of future minimum lease payments (cash outflows) or the fair value is recorded as a liability and an asset in the balance sheet. That asset is depreciated annually. As time goes on, the depreciation and interest payments are recorded as expenses in the income statement. Interest on lease can be calculated as,

Lease payments as beginning of period x interest rate.

In terms of the cash flow statement, the total lease payment is separated into principal and interest payments. When using IFRS, the principal amount goes into investing activities, while interest payments can go into either financing or operating activities. Under US GAAP, the interest amount goes into operating activities, while the principal amount goes into financing activities (as outflows).

Impact of financing vs operating lease on the lessee`s financial statements

	Finance lease	Operating lease
Assets	Higher	Lower
Total liabilities	Higher	Lower
Net income (at inception of lease)	Lower	Higher
Net income (in subsequent years)	Higher	Lower
EBIT	Higher	Lower
Over all net income (in all periods)	Same	Same
Operating cash flow	Higher	Lower
Cash flow from financing	Lower	Higher
Total cash flow	Same	Same

Impact of financing vs operating lease on lessee`s ratios

	Finance lease	Operating lease
Current ratio (CA/CL)	Lower	Higher
Working capital	Lower	Higher

	(CA − CL)		
Asset turnover (Revenue / TA)		Lower	Higher
Return on assets (in early periods) (NI / TA)		Lower	Higher
Return on equity (in early periods) (NI / SE)		Lower	Higher
Debt / Assets		Higher	Lower
Debt / Equity		Higher	Lower

In finance lease all ratios are worse. In financial statements, we see some benefits like EBIT, which is higher (because interest is not subtracted in

EBIT calculation), CFO is higher (because principal repayments go into CFF) and higher net income in subsequent years in the finance lease.

Lessor`s perspective

Under IFRS, the criteria for operating or finance lease are the same for the lessor. However, US GAAP is a little bit different here. Under U.S. GAAP, if any of the criteria of a finance lease are met, plus the collection of lease payments is reasonably certain, then it is a finance lease; otherwise, it is treated as an operating lease.

We know that with an operating lease, the lessor reports rental income and depreciates the leased asset. With a capital lease, the lessor removes the asset (from the balance sheet) and creates a lease investment account as a lease receivable.

Reporting by the Lessor

From the perspective of the lessor, a lease is also classified into one of two categories: 1. Finance lease 2. Operating lease.

Finance lease: When the lease is treated as a finance lease, the lessor removes the asset from the balance sheet. If the lessor is the manufacturer of that asset, then they will recognize the present value of lease payments as the sale price and the cost of the asset as the carrying value. So, the difference between the sale price and the cost of the asset is gross profit (as a normal sale of the asset).

If the lessor is not a manufacturer or dealer but only provides a lease, then the gross profit at the inception of the lease is zero. It means the sale price is recognized as the present value of lease payments. At the inception of the lease, the asset is removed from the balance sheet, and an equal amount of lease receivable (equal to the present value of lease payments) is created. As the lease goes on, the principal amount of the lease received reduces the lease receivable (as the lessor is selling the asset at fair market value and loaning the amount to the lessee). The other part of the lease received (other than principal) is interest, and it is recognized as interest income. In the cash flow statement, interest received goes into CFO, and the principal (lease) reduction goes into CFI as an inflow.

Operating lease: In an operating lease, the lessor treats it as rental income. The lessor keeps the asset in the balance sheet and depreciates it.

Defined contribution vs defined benefit pension plans

Pension: It is the amount of funds collected from employees during their service. These funds are used to support the person after retirement.

The two broad categories of pension plans are defined contribution plans and defined benefit plans.

Defined contribution plan: It is a retirement plan in which the employer contributes a certain amount of money in each period (i.e., monthly) into the employee's retirement account. The contribution may depend on the employee's contribution, the employee's experience, the duration of the employee's service, etc. The employee can also contribute the same or a different amount. The firm provides no promises about the future value of the plan. The money is invested, and it can earn positive or negative earnings. The investment decisions are left to the employee. The employee bears all the risks involved linked to investment.

Financial reporting requirement: Financial reporting requirements for a defined contribution plan are straightforward. Amount contributed by the employer is his pension expense, and there is no future liability to report on the balance sheet.

Defined benefit plan: It is a retirement plan in which the employer assumes the risk of the future value of the plan. The employer promises to pay certain periodic payments to the employee in the future (after retirement). In this plan, the employer contributes a certain amount (the employee may or may not contribute) into a fund and generally sends the amount to an institution that specializes in investment. The employer makes sure of a certain future value of the fund. The retirement benefits usually depend on an employee's years of service or the compensation at retirement. For example, an employee who is entitled to 3% of her salary (of $200000) and served for 30 years may get

200000 x 30 x 2% = $120000

Financial reporting requirement: Financial reporting is complicated here. The employer needs to estimate the value of the future obligation of the defined benefit plan. The variables used to forecast are the mortality rate, future compensation amount (salary), retirement age, and discount rate.

If the fair value of the plan assets is greater than the future obligations, then the plan is called an overfunded plan, and an asset named net pension is to be recorded in the balance sheet of the employer. On the other hand, if the fair value is less than the pension obligation, the plan is called underfunded, and the employer has to record net pension liability in the balance sheet.

Reporting under IFRS

1. Service cost/past service cost + Interest income/ expense go into the Income statement (under pension expense)

3. Re-measurement + Actuarial gains/losses + Actual return + Expected return go into   Balance   sheet   (under shareholders' equity)

Reporting under US GAAP

1. Service cost/past service cost + Interest income/ expense go into the Income statement (under pension expense).
2. Expected return on assets + Actuarial gains/losses go into   Balance   sheet   (under   shareholder's   equity)   (the amortization of expected return on assets + Actuarial gains/losses goes back into income statement as expense.

First, we need to define these terms;

Service cost: It is the present value of the retirement benefits that an employee is entitled to take in the current year.

Past service costs: It is the changes in the value of the defined benefit plan in previous periods. Interest expense or interest income is equal to the value of the asset at the beginning of the year x interest rate.

The interest rate depends on the management`s judgment, but it should reflect the yield rate of an A-rated bond.

Actuarial gains and losses are the difference between the actual pension payments and the expected amount. Actuarial gain = amount paid < expected. Actuarial loss = amount paid > expected.

Under IFRS

Any change in net liability or asset is calculated and annually calculated and reported in financial statements. These changes are recorded in other comprehensive income, in net income, or in the balance sheet. Under IFRS, service cost, interest expense, and expected return on plan assets go into the income statement, and then go to the balance sheet ultimately. On the other hand, past services cost, actuarial gains or losses go into the balance sheet.

Under US GAAP

Under US GAAP there are five parts of net pension asset or liability. Service costs, net interest expense, and the expected return are the components of the net pension expense that go into the income statement.

Past service costs and actuarial gains or losses go into other comprehensive income. These two are amortized into current pension expense annually. It means the firm can report its pension expense and net pension obligation over the term of the life of the plan.

For a manufacturing firm, the IFRS and US GAAP pension expense is allocated to cost of goods sold and inventory (for direct labor) and to administrative expenses and salaries (for administrative services). Therefore, pension expense does not show in the income statement. Footnotes must be examined carefully to understand the pension expense.

Leverage and coverage ratios

Leverage ratios: In leverage ratios, we use balance sheet items to calculate the debt amount in a firm`s capital structure.

Some terms need to be understood first

Total debt: In leverage ratios, total debt means all interest-bearing liabilities (i.e., loans from banks). All other liabilities that do not bear interest are not included, like payables, deferred tax, etc.

Total assets: These are all current and long-term assets.

Total capital= total debt + equity

Average total assets= {total assets in previous year + total assets current year} /2

Average equity= {equity in previous year + equity in current year} /2

Leverage ratios
Debt to assets ratio = total debt / total assets.

It measures the percentage of total assets that are being financed with debt. A percentage of less than 50 is good.

Debt to capital ratio = Total debt / total capital

It is a measure of the percentage of total capital financed by debt.

Debt to equity ratio = total debt / total equity.

It measures the amount of debt financing relative to the firm's equity financing. If this ratio is 1, it means the firm has equal amounts of debt and equity. Means 50 % capital came from equity, and the other 50% from debt.

Financial leverage ratio = average total assets / average total equity.

It measures how much assets a company has relative to its equity. The higher the ratio, the higher the leverage and riskier the firm is.

All the leverage ratios must be lower than or equal to the industry norms. A higher ratio of any of these ratios means higher leverage and more risk.

Coverage ratios

With coverage ratios, we use the income statement element to measure the adequacy of earnings to cover fixed charges like interest payments.

Interest coverage ratio = EBIT / interest payments.

A higher ratio is desirable. If this ratio is lower, then the firm is experiencing difficulty in interest payments.

Fixed charge coverage ratio = (EBIT + lease payments) / (interest payments + lease payments).

This is like an interest coverage ratio, but also considers lease payments too. It should also be higher.

Chapter 11: Financial reporting quality

Financial reporting quality: Financial reporting quality is the usefulness of a financial document/set of financial documents for those who need to make decisions about the firm.
Generally, users of financial documents are investors, creditors, potential business partners, etc.
Financial documents are useful if they fulfill the following conditions
- Relevance
- Timeliness
- Faithful representation.

Relevance means the information generated by financial documents must impact the decision-making of users of these documents. Relevance also means the information must be material.

Timeliness means the information must be provided in time when the users need to make decisions about the company.

Faithful representation means completeness, neutrality, and the absence of errors.

Quality of reported results: It means sustainability and the level of earnings. How sustainable is the business in producing this level of earnings? Higher earnings due to the events which are not likely to occur (like changes in exchange rate) in the future do not mean a sustainable level of earnings. On the other hand, attaining efficiency and reduction in cost may lead to sustainability. A higher level of earnings means that earnings are high enough to fulfill operational needs as well as a decent return to investors.

A higher quality of financial reporting may not guarantee a higher quality of reported results. Higher quality means the financial documents are GAAP-compliant but may not be sustainable.

Assessing financial reporting quality

We can gauge the quality of financial reporting and the quality of reported results from worst to best.

Lowest quality financial reports: The lowest quality reports may contain fictitious entries. These are the entries that did not occur in reality but have been added intentionally to mislead users of reports. These reports are also non-GAAP compliant.

Going up from worst reporting comes the **noncompliance reporting:** These reports may contain partially fictitious information, but do not obey the generally accepted accounting standards. These reports may overstate or understate some items, contain improper calculations, and include estimates of assets and liabilities.

GAAP-compliant reports: These reports are GAAP-compliant, but management is using those estimates or methods (Intentionally or unintentionally) that lead to the creation of biased reports. Biasness reduces the usability of reports, and users can conclude inaccurate future estimates. Biases can be aggressive (inflated results), conservative, or smoothening (to show smooth results by reducing earnings in better situations to offset bad earnings in other periods, being conservative in years of good performance, and being aggressive in years of poor performance).

Reports that are GAAP compliant, decision useful but not sustainable.

It means earnings may not be expected to continue into the future and are from non-recurring activities.

GAAP compliant, decision useful and sustainable reports: It means that the reports comply with the accounting standards of the company's jurisdiction, the reports are relevant verifiable understandable and delivered in a timely manner, and earnings reported are from activities which were expected to continue into the future.

Conservative vs aggressive accounting

The unbiased and neutral financial documents are more valuable in the view of an analyst (and for other users). It means management neither uses conservative accounting nor aggressive accounting.

Conservative accounting: In conservative accounting, the management tends to decrease the firm's current earnings and financial position, resulting in reports of less income and a weaker financial position. Use of conservatism, the tendency of future earnings increases.

Aggressive accounting: If management decides to increase current earnings and financial position, it is called aggressive accounting. In this method, the future earnings tend to decrease.

Both aggressive and conservative accounting is not desirable. Both of these are biased and used by management to smooth their earnings (and reduce volatility) over several years.

The following are some examples of conservative vs aggressive accounting (based on management's choices and estimates)

Aggressive	Conservative
Capitalizing cost (so the earnings would be higher)	Expensing costs (so the earnings would be lower)
More useful life of assets (less depreciation expense, higher net income)	Less useful life of assets (higher depreciation less net income)
Higher salvage value (less depreciation)	Lower estimates of salvage value (more depreciation)
Declining balance or straight-line depreciation	Double accelerating depreciation method
Higher accruals of receivables (fewer bad debts)	Less receivable estimates (more bad debts)
Late impairment recognition	Early recognition of impairment

Motives and conditions to issue low-quality and fraudulent financial statements

There are three things that led management to produce low-quality or even fraudulent reports,
Opportunity
Motivation
Rationalization

1. Opportunity: When management is given an opportunity, they might take it. It mostly happens when internal controls are weak, the board is ineffective, or a lack of fear of punishment.

2. Motivations: There are many motivations for management to produce low-quality reports. For example, when a manager is trying to maintain business competitiveness by hiding a period of poor performance.

Earnings have been the most important measure in the eyes of management in terms of setting targets. Beating prior years or analysts' expectations is a very common goal.

Sometimes the motivation is to avoid a penalty from a debt covenant's perspective.

3. **Rationalization:** By rationalization, we mean that a person is interested in justifying their fraudulent or biased decisions.

The management seeks opportunities to justify or defend their actions. So, they believe that their choices are either in their own self-interest or in the interests of those they intend to support.

Mechanisms to discipline financial reporting quality and their limits

There are four mechanisms that contribute to the level of quality of a company's financial reports.
- Market forces and investor expectations.
- Regulatory authorities.
- Auditors
- Private contracting.

Market forces and investor expectations: We know that a company's cost of capital depends on the business risks and investors' expectations of the risk. When a company produces low-quality reports, the expectation of risk is increased, and investors will demand a higher rate of return in order to invest or lend in that company. So, the cost of capital increases. On the other hand, by persistently producing higher-quality reports, the cost of capital would be reduced.

Sometimes here, a conflict of interest arises. Management wants to reduce the cost of capital, but they might have an incentive to produce low-quality reports.

Regulatory authorities: There are several authorities around the globe to establish and enforce rules and standards to protect market participants. **For example,** in Europe, the European Securities and Markets Authority, the Financial Conduct Authority (FCA) in the UK, and the Securities and Exchange Commission (SEC)7 in the USA.

Along these, there are many regional regulators and members of the IOSCO, the international organization of securities commissions, the global standard setter for the securities sector.

These authorities have a number of ways to influence and implement higher quality in financial reporting. For example,

Registration requirements: This means that companies must become transparent before offering securities. These regulatory authorities are a first step check on the company.

Disclosure requirements: There are several documents and their contents that a company is required to submit. Regulatory authorities have rules for these submissions and disclosures regarding those submissions.

Auditing regulators: These regulators ask the company to obtain unqualified reports of independent auditors to ensure best accounting practices.

Enforcement power of regulator: Regulatory authorities have the power to fine and suspend companies for any wrongdoing.

A limitation is to be discussed here. If a regulator is not strong enough, it may not be able to ensure high-quality reports to the users.

Auditors: This is the simplest of the four mechanisms. When an independent auditor clears the financial documents, the users get some assurance that the proper methods of estimates, disclosures, and related accounting standards have been followed.

Regrettably, the work of an auditor is limited. It is limited to the information provided to the auditor. If management deliberately misleads the auditor, the auditor`s report might also be misleading.

Mostly, an auditor`s opinion is based on a sample of accounts. If the fraud is hidden in depth, it might be hard for an auditor to detect.

The auditors do not seek out fraudulent activity intentionally. They use a designated set of processes to check if the reports are accounting standard-compliant and fair.

Private contracting: Private contracting parties are another important source for financial discipline. For example, a lending party would calculate different financial measures and come up with better interpretations. Parties that do business with a particular company have an incentive to look closely at their business affairs.

A limitation here is that when there is a penalty from lenders for certain events, like lower earnings, the borrower has some incentive to produce low-quality reports.

Presentation choices are used to influence an analyst`s opinion.

Accounting choices (in the calculation and presentation of financial data) made in financial reporting must be understood by analysts in order to evaluate a company's financial reports. These choices affect the usefulness of reports.

Sometimes firms use some measures not defined in GAAP or not required in GAAP to make financial reports better. Normally, these are excluded from financial reports. Justifications given by management for this exclusion include

- These items are of non-recurring
- They are non-cash items
- By excluding these items, they are improving comparability.

In the US, the firms that use non-GAAP measures are required to disclose the following

Show the most comparable GAAP measure with the same prominence

Give a justification for why the non-GAAP measure is useful

Reconcile/ ratify the difference between non-GAAP and comparable GAAP measures

Purpose of using non-GAAP measures

IFRS requires the following to be disclosed for using non-IFRS measures

Relevance of such a measure

Reconcile the difference between non-IFRS and the most comparable IFRS measure

Here is an example of a non-GAAP measure from which you will have quite an idea.

A company is downsizing and expensing much on it. They may exclude these expenses and show more information on operations to paint a good picture.

Choices of accounting methods and estimates that could be used to manage earnings, cash flow, and balance sheet items

There are various ways in which management can change results and show better results in their financial reports. Through these methods, they can affect the balance sheet, income statement, and cash flows.

Some of these methods are used to gear up a below normal performance, and others can reduce the results.

Choices affecting the balance sheet: We must be looking in
- Revenue recognition.
- Inventory management.
- Accrual accounting
- Deferred tax assets.
- Depreciation.
- Capitalization of expenses.

Revenue recognition: It means management is recognizing revenues early or delaying them according to their need.

For example, we have a huge order to export goods at the end of the period. We need to recognize the earnings when the title and responsibilities of ordered goods have been transferred. But in order to make things look better, management decides to recognize the revenues before the end of the period (and before the transfer of responsibility), they are influencing the revenues for the current period.

Inventory: How the management is recording the cost of goods sold and ending inventory in the accounts.

We have three methods: FIFO first in, first out, weighted average cost, and LIFO (last in, first out.

When prices are going up, use of FIFO gives us out-of-date cost of goods sold but a better inventory in hand (inventory value is according to current market prices). This makes the balance sheet look better.

By using the weighted average method, the cost of goods sold is somewhat closer to the current fair value, but the balance sheet is not as close to the current market value of inventory (as it was with the use of FIFO). Management has the opportunity here to engineer the balance sheet according to its needs.

LIFO is not permitted under IFRS, so let`s not discuss it here, as we have discussed it in detail before. I think we got the idea of how the inventory method can be used by management to their advantage.

Accrual accounting: It is a method of reporting current period activity as opposed to current period cash. It means revenues and expenses should be recognized when they occur, irrespective of whether cash may or may not change hands.

Management can use this approach to their advantage to manipulate results. When a firm sells the goods, they have receivables. They need to maintain a provision for bad debts and the fair value of collectibles. These two items are subject to the judgment of management.

Deferred tax assets: After experiencing a loss, the management creates an account of deferred tax assets in its balance sheet. When will they be in profit they will use that deferred tax asset to reduce their tax bill. This is true for startup companies and the successful companies that hit a loss accidentally. But what if a company is in decline and will be going out of business in the next four or five years, they may not use their entire deferred tax asset. This is also a subjective approach and is at management`s discretion.

Depreciation methods: It is an allocation of the cost of a long-lived asset over several years.

There are three major methods.
- Straight line.
- Accelerated
- Activity-based.

And we also have to estimate salvage value.

The choice of depreciation method and estimates about salvage value depend on management. The different choice may lead to different results.

Capitalization: It means the firm has to decide whether the expense they made is going to give them a benefit in one year or in multiple years. Sometimes management delays the current expenses by capitalizing them to show better earnings in the current period.

Accounting choices to influence the statement of cash flow

Statement of cash flow has three parts
- CFO, operating cash flows.
- CFI, cash flows from investment activities.
- CFF, cash flow from financing activities.

Within the cash flow statement, the CFO is of the most importance to check the earnings of the firm. With respect to accruals and depreciation, cash flows are less likely to be manipulated.

First of all, we need to check the relationship between net income and operating cash flow.

If the amount of cash generated in a period > net income, we have good quality earnings and financial reports.

If the amount of cash generated in a period < net income, we have bad quality earnings and financial reports.

When cash inflow is far lower than net earnings, it means management did something to report higher earnings than the actual reality.

The company management knows a lower inflow from operations will look bad, so they also use some methods to raise cash inflow. The most common way of doing this is by managing accounts payable. What if management wants to show more cash in hand by delaying payment to their supplier? They will be raising accounts payable, but the cash position would be higher. They can fool us if we only see at cash position and ignore payables.

Sometimes management decides to show improved cash flow by **misclassifying items** from investing or financing activities. In this method, they bring inflow items into the CFO. Sometimes, management constructs a complex transaction/agreement to confuse the user, which is also a bad sign.

Accounting warning signs and methods for detecting manipulation in financial reports

In this part, we will be looking at
- Revenues,
- Inventory,
- Capitalization,
- Relationship between net income and cash flow,
- Fourth quarter earnings
- Non-recurring entries.

Revenues: This is the item that is the number one source of manipulation. So, we have to look at this item first. First of all, we need to look at the notes for management policies regarding revenue recognition, rebates, etc. Any suspicious entry here would be a bad start

If a company has outperformed compared to its peers and competitors, we need to check it. Is this performance achieved through superior management, superior product, or through manipulation?

If the firm has outperformed or deviated from its historical trends, we need to check for a reasonable explanation.

After that, we need to check ratios like receivables turnover, days sales outstanding, and asset turnover, and compare them to the industry norms.

Inventory: The firms that hold inventory have significant opportunities to manipulate it. We must check and compare the inventory figures with industry norms and the company's own historical trends. Anything unusual must be checked for a reasonable explanation.

Inventory turnover ratios must also be checked. A declining inventory turnover might indicate a threat of obsolescence. We should compare it with industry norms and the company's historical trends, and provide a reasonable explanation.

Capitalization: It also means deferring of costs. First of all, check the notes regarding policies relating to capitalization. Compare these policies with industry norms. If a difference appears, check out asset turnover and profitability ratios for comparability.

Relationship between net income and cash flow: Cash inflows play a very critical role for a company to perform well and even to survive. When a firm is aggressively capitalizing costs (meaning delaying costs as expenses), they are showing higher income for the current period. The same results can also be achieved by aggressive accrual accounting. If cash is not coming in despite higher earnings, it must get the analyst into suspicion. We need to calculate the percentage of cash inflow with respect to income (cash inflow/ income) over a number of years to see the trends. If the cash inflow percentage declines, it's a red flag, and the analyst must demand or seek further investigation.

Fourth quarter earnings: We need to look at 4th quarter earnings. Do they match the previous quarter's earnings or not? (Of course we must consider the element of seasonality).

Non-recurring or one-off items: We need to look closely for non-recurring items if they recur again and again, and vice versa. For example, a huge cash inflow from a non-recurring item is stated in income from operations, and an expense is stated in non-recurring expense, but comes into accounts several times.

Chapter 12:
Financial Statement Analysis:
Applications

Evaluation of a company's past financial performance and strategies

In the evaluation of past performance, we are interested in how things have changed with the passage of time. We not only check how the firm has performed but are also interested in why (poor or better).

In performance evaluation, first of all, we need to think about trend analysis regarding profitability, efficiency, liquidity, and solvency, as well as any reason why they have changed.

Then, this trend must be compared with the industry (peers and competitors). If this firm is performing differently in comparison, then why?

Secondly, we need to understand the factors that lead to success in this industry and where this firm stands.

Thirdly, what is the model of this firm, its competitive strategy, and how management is able to grow profitability and increase efficiency.

To answer all the above-mentioned questions, we need to look at the company's financial statements, disclosures, and proxies, like the investor relations department, Corporate press releases, and related information that analysts can get by visiting the company. We must also look at industry information, trade surveys, publications, etc.

After getting all the information, we perform various analysis tools like

- Common-size financial statements.
- Financial ratios
- Compare with industry-specific metrics.

After performing the analysis tool, we need to understand and conclude.

For example, if our firm under consideration is in the business of premium products, they must be selling at a high profit margin and lower cost of goods sold, higher research and development costs, etc. So, all these elements must be seen in the financial statements of our firm.

Forecasting a company's future net income and cash flows

Reason for future projection: Projections of a company's cash flows are used for credit analysis. The most common users of these projections are future and current lenders and or partners to understand the company's default risk.

Data: The data would be internal (the company's financial statements), industrial outlook, and macro-economic variables, etc.

Past performance is very useful in terms of a guide to forecast the future for a stable and well-diversified company. But a company with a volatile and new company's past performance may not be a very useful item to consider.

We generally have two types of future forecasts

- Short-term/near-term
- Long-term/multi-period

First of all, we must forecast the company`s sales. To forecast sales, we use <u>a top-down approach in short-term</u> projections.

With this approach first, we forecast industry sales revenue. We use regression analysis to build a relationship between industry overall sales revenue and some macro indicators like real GDP. With the industry sales forecast, we forecast our company`s sales revenues by considering our company`s share in the market. If the future market share of the company we are taking into consideration is going to change, we need to adjust it too.

Next, we forecast expenses. (Sometimes we avoid expense forecasting and go directly for gross profit margin by historical trends; historical trends are more useful in well-diversified and stable companies.)

To forecast net profit, we need to consider financial leverage and tax effects. We can also forecast net profit margin (like gross profit, but with the same disadvantage).

In any kind of forecast, beware of the following items like
Non-recurring or discontinued items must be excluded from analysis.

Restructuring charges must be ignored.

Because if we include them in the model, we are expecting them to happen again, but this is not true.

Multi-period forecast: In this forecast, we use a single estimate of the growth rate and use it to forecast future items. For example, we use 5% for sales and use it for future sales revenues.

To estimate future cash flows, we need to make some assumptions about uses and sources of cash.

By building a multi-period forecast, we end up as follows

Income and cashflow projections

	2x10 current	2x11	2x12	2x13
Sale @4%	1200	1248	1297.9	1349.8
Less COGS @5%	600	630	661.5	694.58
Less opearting expenses@3%	200	206	212.18	218.55
Net income	400	412	424.24	436.72
Opening cash@2%	200	204	208.08	212.24
Net income	400	412	424.24	436.72
Non cash items (working capital)@75% of sales	900	936	973.44	1012.4
Ending cash	**1500**	**1552**	**1605.8**	**1661.3**

Role of financial statement analysis in assessing the credit quality of a debt investment

Credit analysis is an evaluation of credit risk. It is an analysis of an entity's ability to pay its debts.

Analysts include 3Cs, 4Cs, and 5Cs for credit analysis. 3Cs include character (firm`s history and reputation regarding debt payments), collateral (type of asset as collateral), and Capacity to repay (examination of financial statements and ratios). In 4Cs, all of the above, plus capital (the firm`s financial resources) are included. In 5Cs, one more item is included in the above four, which is "conditions" (special conditions applicable to debt).

We know that debt must be repaid in cash. Analysts focus on the multi-period cash flow forecast, especially the CFO, because debt is to be paid from internally generated cash.

Moody's, Standard and Poor's, and other credit rating companies established some formulas to rate a firm`s credibility regarding debt repayment. These formulas include a weighted average of some ratios and business characteristics. The items included in the formula and their weight differs from industry to industry, but they can be categorized as under:

- Scaling and diversification.
- Tolerance for leverage
- Margin stability
- Operational efficiency

Scaling and diversification: In this category, we are to look at a firm`s ability to withstand adverse economic or business conditions/events. If they have more control over suppliers and in the market, they have less credit risk.

Tolerance for leverage: In this, we include the interest coverage ratio and the ratio of debt to total assets. A firm having better of these ratios means they have higher tolerance and lower credit risk.

Operational efficiency: Items like Return on Assets and costs are included in this section. A higher return and or lower costs are better for lower credit risk.

Margin stability: It is related to variations in profit margins. The lower the variation, the higher the credit rating (lower credit risk).

We have discussed credit quality in detail in fixed income risk analysis.

Use of financial statement analysis in the assessment of equity investments

Screening means selecting a suitable portfolio from a large set of stocks. Selection may involve calculations and comparing ratios.

First thing to think about is what type of investment we are looking for from growth stocks, value stocks, or dividend earnings stocks.

Analysts use some ratios to select stocks. Multiple criteria must be used to select a stock, for example, a low price to earnings ratio is desirable, but a firm can have a lower price to earnings ratio if they have declining sales or are very highly leveraged.

By testing the firms using historical data and ratios from that data, analysts must be aware of the biases and limitations of ratios. If these biases exist, the results cannot be trusted.

Survivorship bias: The tendency to focus only on winners rather than losers is called survivorship bias. For example, when we are looking for a better investment fund, we include only those funds that have survived to date. Maybe a large number of funds have been closed due to bad performance or bitter situations. It means we are overemphasizing a single fund and ignoring all others. This bias gives us results we cannot rely on.

Look-ahead bias: This type of bias occurs when specific data is used to test a relationship, but the data was not available at that point in time. For example, while calculating price to book value for studying trading strategies, the price is available at any point in time, but the book value is available after 30 to 60 days after the end of the accounting period. One other example is restated financial statements. When the screening process was done, the restated figures were not available.

Data snooping bias: This is another statistical bias, and it occurs when the same data is used to test a model that was used to build that model. According to statisticians, this type of bias cannot be fully eliminated.

Adjustments in Financial statements to compare different companies

Most of the time, analysts make some adjustments in the financial statements of different companies that use different accounting choices and estimates so the statements can become comparison-friendly. The difference in financial statements occurs because different companies choose different accounting methods and or different accounting standards.

Investments in securities: Buying equity and other debt offerings of other companies is called investments in securities. It does not mean equity interests of the parent company in the subsidiary firm.

The management can classify investment in securities in three categories, which can affect the net income differently.

These categories are
- Held for trading.
- Available for sale.
- Hold to maturity.

Held for trading:

If these securities are held for trading, they must be measured at fair value, and their unrealized gains and losses are reported in the income statement, under US GAAP.

Available for sale:
Hold to maturity:

Under these categories, the securities are measured at fair value, and unrealized gains/losses are recorded in other comprehensive income in the balance sheet.

A problem arises when firms choose to classify similar securities differently. So, the analyst has to make some adjustments based on the accounting treatment for each type. Undoing the effect of one classification would make financial statements more comparable.

There is one other difference that arises from the choice of accounting standard (IFRS vs US GAAP). If the interest rate fluctuates and there is an unrealized gain/loss on held-for-sale securities. Under IFRS, this unrealized gain/loss would be recorded in the income statement. But under US GAAP, that would not be the case. So, this difference would be eliminated by adding losses or subtracting gains from the income statement of an IFRS firm.

Inventory: The Choice of accounting treatment for inventory produces different financial results. We have FIFO, weighted average cost, and LIFO (only under US GAAP) methods for inventory management.

The problem arises when one company operating under US GAAP chooses LIFO while another company under IFRS chooses weighted average or FIFO. This choice of using different inventory methods has effects on COGS and profit margins. It also affects total assets in the balance sheet and equity.

Fortunately, any company reporting under the LIFO method is required to disclose the value of its inventory equivalent to the FIFO base. We just need to consult management's notes.

Depreciation: Like inventory, the choice of depreciation method also has drastic effects on financial statements both the income statement and the balance sheet). There are three elements related to depreciation that are in management's discretion.
- Schedule/method of depreciation
- Useful life of the asset.
- Salvage value of the asset.

Schedule/method of depreciation: We have
Straight line method: depreciation is spread equally over the useful life of the asset.
Accelerated method: Higher depreciation in the early years of the useful life of the asset.
Usage-based method: Higher allocation of depreciation in the higher production season.
Useful life: The higher the useful life management estimates, the lower the depreciation expense.
Salvage value: The Higher the salvage value estimates, the lower the depreciation and vice versa.

We need to adjust depreciation expense so that our understanding of the company's depreciation expense improves, and we would be able to compare it with other companies.
Unfortunately, from the financial statements and disclosures, we would not have enough information about the assets and their depreciation. This is also because the assets

are shown in aggregation and are in different stages of their useful life.

We can use some ratios to find some information about assets. For example, the useful life of a company's asset = accumulated depreciation / gross property, plant, and equipment.

Number of years of depreciation expense that has been recognized so far = Accumulated depreciation /current depreciation expense. Useful life remaining on the overall asset = net property, plant, and equipment/depreciation expense. Average life of assets and installation = Gross property plant and equipment /depreciation expense.

There is another difference worth mentioning. US GAAP does not allow upward valuation of fixed assets, but it is permitted under IFRS. So, if a company reporting under IFRS and valued an asset upward, we need to reverse the upward valuation effect to compare it with a company operating under US GAAP.

Goodwill: Goodwill arises when a company acquires another company and pays more than the fair value of the acquired assets. Goodwill goes into the balance sheet as an asset and is tested annually and written down if impaired.

There is a problem of comparison between two companies, with one having grown by acquisition and the other having grown internally. The acquiring firm records goodwill by capitalizing the extra payment on acquisition, while an internally growing company normally expends its growth expenditures. So how do we compare them?

We can remove goodwill, other intangible assets (from the balance sheet), and Impairment charges (from the income statement). This will give us a better comparable view, and ratios would make more sense, and must also be removed from the income statement.

Off-balance sheet financing: Capital lease (Finance lease) and its future payments are recorded in financial statements. Operation lease is not recorded, but as we know, it is an essential mode of financing, and it must be considered while calculating ratios, especially when comparing two companies, one with capital, while the other with an operating lease. We must calculate the present value of future expected operating lease payments to get a better comparison with the firm using a finance lease. Let's do it with the help of an example.

The following data is given.

Year	Capital lease	Operating lease
2X12	$200000	$400000
2X13	$200000	$400000
2X14	$200000	$400000
2X15	$200000	$400000
Beyond 2X15	$800000	$900000

Present value of capital lease is $700000

To calculate present value, we need a discount rate. For discount rate and other calculations, we have two methods.

1. **Assume the operating lease has the same ratio of present value to payments as the firm's capital lease.**

A total of $1600000 of capital lease and a total of $2500000 of operating lease is to be paid in the future.

Ratio of present value (of capital lease) to future payments = $\frac{700000}{1600000} = 0.4573$

Using this, we can estimate the PV of the operating lease as,
PV of operating lease = 0.4573*2500000 =$1093750

2. **Estimate the discount rate for the capital lease and apply it to the operating lease.**

To have a single discount rate for capital lease, we have to have some assumptions, like we assume the capital lease to be fully paid in 6 or 7 years, etc. If we assume the total years of payment are 6, then we can find IRR, which gives us PV equal to $700000. That IRR would be used for an operating lease.

That's all for FRA. I wish the best of luck to all students. You can share your opinion to make this book better

You can also check other books in the investment series (click on the following links)

Economics for investment IN ONE WEEK

Fixed Income IN ONE WEEK

Derivative and Alternative Investment

Equity investment for CFA Level 1

www.ingramcontent.com/pod-product-compliance
Lightning Source LLC
Chambersburg PA
CBHW030627220526
45463CB00004B/1438